Edw. G. Melville

J. C. Scott

Douglas Forest

[signature]

Pat Dollan

[signature]

James Barr

James G. Le Vean

[signature], Col USAF.

[signature]

Allan Young

Ernest W. Drew

[signature]

[signature]

[signature]

SONGS OF LIBERTY

ROBERT BURNS

Born at Alloway, 1759
Died at Dumfries, 1796

The text followed in this selection is
that of the complete edition of
Burns's poetical works edited by Charles
Dougall, now temporarily out of print.
The glossary is from the same source.

SONGS OF LIBERTY

BY

ROBERT BURNS

A SELECTION BY
SIR PATRICK DOLLAN, LL.D.

ADAM & CHARLES BLACK
4, 5 & 6 SOHO SQUARE LONDON W.1
1944

FIRST PUBLISHED 1943, REPRINTED 1944
THIS BOOK IS PRODUCED IN COMPLETE CONFORMITY
WITH THE AUTHORIZED ECONOMY STANDARDS

To the Memory of
PTE. BOB M'KIM
K.O.S.B.
Killed at Dunkirk, June 1940

MADE IN GREAT BRITAIN
PRINTED BY MORRISON AND GIBB LTD., LONDON AND EDINBURGH

Introduction

No man fought more bravely against tyranny, despotism and dictatorship at home and abroad than Robert Burns. By nature a lover of fellowship and peace and a hater of strife and war, he realised that fellowship and peace were impossible without personal freedom, national independence and international security. He believed in the God-given right of every man to pray, work and govern, and was among the first to proclaim the stupidity of poverty in the midst of plenty.

He could have attained to a life of ease and luxury by sacrificing his principles and compromising with pomp and privilege but he preferred to live as a free man and, therefore, not remote from hardship and criticism. Robert Burns in his own life realised the truth of the biblical philosophy that no man made profit for his own mind by gaining the world but losing his soul.

He proclaimed the rights of man in the days of his youth and understood the spiritual meaning of the American War of Independence and the French Revolution. He championed the cause of freedom in speech and in writing for every citizen, and denounced oppression and hypocrisy without regard to consequence. He dared to be free in speech and writing at a time when it was dangerous for the ordinary man, as he was, to express opinions on politics, religion and philosophy.

Democracy was not recognised in his own country when he was challenging every convention and privilege and asserting the right of every citizen to have a say in the making and unmaking of governments and in the framing and amendment of laws.

He wrote " Scots, Wha Hae " not as a boastful glorification of the Scottish victory at Bannockburn, but as a clarion call to the men of all nations to rise in their might against tyrants in whatever walk of life they robbed and plundered sheepfolds and granaries. " Scots, Wha Hae " is the hymn of free men the world over, and represents after one hundred and fifty years what the men and women of the United Nations are fighting for in their struggle to destroy the dictatorship and aggression of the Nazis and Fascists whether German, Italian, Japanese or any other brand, for all time.

He who took up the sword against tyranny in his own land understood that it could not be tolerated in any other country without its becoming a danger to his own land, himself, and other advocates of liberty. That was why, when the French Revolution was exploited for ambitions of military dictatorship, he made his declaration for British Unity in " Does Haughty Gaul Invasion Threat." He was conscious of the wrongs that he and millions of others suffered in his own country, but he knew that British wrongs could best be righted by British hands. It was imperative, therefore, that Britons who believed in freedom at home and abroad should unite for the time and prevent a foreign foe rallying on British soil. The fight against native injustices could be resumed later.

It was in the same manifesto that he sang the principles of Constitutional Monarchy that have since become so interwoven in our way of government that we think of the King and People as co-partners in the onward march for reform and progress.

There can be no doubt that the Robert Burns who helped to forge the unity of his country against Napoleonic invasion, if he were alive to-day, would be among the foremost in the fight against the poisonous systems of Hitlerism and Fascism.

His message is as true for Democrats in 1943 as when first published.

That is why his poems and songs are so beloved in many lands. He still voices the aspirations of the decent folk who believe that the world can be liberated from war and poverty by a policy of commonsense and good will.

Josef Sladek, the Bohemian poet, who translated Burns seventy years ago said the Scot was the singer of freedom whose love of liberty swept through the universe with stirring and uplifted appeal and inspired millions in lands he never knew. Abraham Lincoln, the great President of America, a few years earlier than Sladek had been influenced by Robert Burns in much the same way. It was from Burns he got much of his guidance on the basic principles of Democracy.

The world now is engaged in a life and death struggle between Democracy and Dictatorship because men in Germany, Italy and Japan have preferred the evil way of domination by dictators rather than use the philosophy of Burns to base government on the goodwill and understanding of the people. When the present struggle is ended by the defeat of Dictatorship, the world will be more ready than ever before to accept the teachings and principles of Robert Burns and endeavour, honestly, to put them into operation.

He set down the creed of Democracy for every man to understand in " A Man's a Man for a' That " in which he has helped all of us to see the need for world brotherhood as the real bulwark against war and want. Long before presidents and prime ministers did, Robert Burns realised the need for world security and tried with all his power to broadcast his message so that it would be understood in every town.

But he knew that this world freedom must arise from personal liberty for every citizen, conditioned by non-interference with neighbours, industrial and economic protection for the home and family and national independence.

He knew the value of understanding nationalism as a foundation for internationalism. Love of country was with him the gateway to world fraternity.

His songs of manliness, of love, of home and of toil are all influenced by the belief that men must work, but need not want as a result.

Not even Sir William Beveridge has lambasted poverty and unemployment as Robert Burns did in " Man Was Made to Mourn " and a " Cotter's Saturday Night." The first is the most eloquent plea in the English language for the right to work for the able-bodied and for the maintenance of the aged when they are no longer able to fend for themselves. The virtues, joys and advantages of home life as we know it in the British Commonwealth have not been better stated in any sermon or oration than in the " Cotter's Saturday Night."

The books about Robert Burns have been published in legions. The call is for still more. Over 100,000 copies of his poems were printed and sold each year prior to the outbreak of this catastrophic war. The demand for his writings since then has been phenomenal, and it has been difficult for the printers and publishers to maintain an adequate supply.

The selection of his poems which I have made is in response to appeals from servicemen and civilians of our own and other nationalities. It is an attempt to illustrate what Robert Burns meant by Democracy, social security, home and fellowship and world fraternity. No writer is capable of influencing the success of world Democracy more than Robert Burns. That is why I believe his poems should be taught in every school.

The late Private Robert M'Kim of the K.O.S.B., killed in the last rearguard action at Dunkirk, was in the 51st Division near Metz behind the Maginot Line when the German mechanised avalanche tore like fury through France. He had written me early in 1940 complaining of standstill tactics and expressing a wish for a war of movement. He suggested that a small collection of the songs of Robert Burns should be compiled for men like himself who wanted to sing their own songs in the battle for freedom rather than the temporary taratiddles of commercialised syncopation. Such a collection was made, and over 10,000 copies distributed amongst the troops of the United Nations.

Most of the songs loved by Robert M'Kim are included in this anthology which may help fighters for freedom at home and abroad to be ever vigilant and fearless in the cause of Liberty and Democracy.

P. J. D.

Contents

I

The Fight for Freedom

II

In Praise of Women

III

Songs of Work

IV

Songs of Fellowship

V

The Fireside and Nature

xi

VI

Religion and Philosophy

VII

Politics and Security

THE FIGHT FOR FREEDOM

The Dumfries Volunteers

Does haughty Gaul invasion threat ?
  Then let the loons beware, Sir,
There's Wooden Walls upon our seas,
  And Volunteers on shore, Sir.
The Nith shall run to Corsincon,
  And Criffel sink in Solway,
Ere we permit a foreign foe
  On British ground to rally !
        We'll ne'er permit, etc.

O let us not like snarling tykes
  In wrangling be divided ;
Till, slap ! come in an unco loon,
  And wi' a rung decide it.
Be Britain still to Britain true,
  Amang oursels united ;
For never but by British hands
  Maun British wrangs be righted !
        No ! never but, etc.

The kettle o' the Kirk and State,
  Perhaps a clout may fail in't ;
But deil a foreign tinkler loon
  Shall ever ca' a nail in't.
Our fathers' bluid the kettle bought,
  And wha wad dare to spoil it ;
By Heaven ! the sacrilegious dog
  Shall fuel be to boil it !
        By Heaven ! etc.

The wretch that wad a tyrant own,
  And the wretch, his true-born brother,
Who would set the mob aboon the throne,
  May they be damned together !

Who will not sing, "God save the King,"
   Shall hang as high's the steeple;
But while we sing, "God save the King,"
   We'll ne'er forget the People!
      But while we sing, etc.

Scots, wha hae

BANNOCKBURN

Robert Bruce's Address to his Army

Scots, wha hae wi' Wallace bled,
Scots, wham Bruce has aften led;
Welcome to your gory bed,
   Or to victorie!

Now's the day, and now's the hour;
See the front o' battle lower;
See approach proud Edward's power—
   Chains and slavery!

Wha will be a traitor knave?
Wha can fill a coward's grave?
Wha sae base as be a slave?
   Let him turn and flee!

Wha for Scotland's King and law
Freedom's sword will strongly draw,
Free-man stand, or free-man fa'?
   Let him on wi' me!

By Oppression's woes and pains!
By your sons in servile chains!
We will drain our dearest veins,
   But they *shall* be free!

Lay the proud Usurpers low!
Tyrants fall in every foe!
Liberty's in every blow!
   Let us do—or die!

The Altar of Independence

TO INDEPENDENCE, AT KERROUGHTRY, SEAT OF MR. HERON,
WRITTEN IN SUMMER, 1794

THOU of an independent mind,
With soul resolv'd, with soul resign'd ;
Prepar'd Power's proudest frown to brave,
Who wilt not be, nor have a slave ;
Virtue alone who dost revere,
Thy own reproach alone dost fear,
Approach this shrine, and worship here.

Written in a Lady's Pocket-Book

GRANT me, indulgent Heaven, that I may live
To see the miscreants feel the pains they give !
Deal Freedom's sacred treasures free as air,
Till slave and despot be but things that were !

I'll go and be a Sodger

EXTEMPORE. APRIL, 1782

O WHY the deuce should I repine,
   And be an ill foreboder ?
I'm twenty-three, and five feet nine—
   I'll go and be a sodger.

I gat some gear wi' meikle care,
   I held it weel thegither ;
But now it's gane and something mair,
   I'll go and be a sodger.

The Silver Tassie of my Bonnie Mary

Go fetch to me a pint o' wine,
   An' fill it in a silver tassie ;
That I may drink before I go,
   A service to my bonnie lassie.
The boat rocks at the pier o' Leith ;
   Fu' loud the wind blaws frae the Ferry ;
The ship rides by the Berwick Law,
   And I maun leave my bonnie Mary.

3

The trumpets sound, the banners fly
　　The glittering spears are ranked ready ;
The shouts o' war are heard afar,
　　The battle closes deep and bloody ;
It's not the roar o' sea or shore
　　Wad mak me langer wish to tarry ;
Nor shout o' war that's heard afar,—
　　It's leaving thee, my bonnie Mary.

The Bonnie Lad that's far awa'

O how can I be blythe and glad,
　　Or how can I gang brisk and braw,
When the bonnie lad that I lo'e best
　　Is o'er the hills and far awa ?

It's no the frosty winter wind,
　　It's no the driving drift and snaw ;
But aye the tear comes in my e'e,
　　To think on him that's far awa.

My father pat me frae his door,
　　My friends they hae disown'd me a' :
But I hae ane will tak my part,
　　The bonnie lad that's far awa.

A pair o' gloves he bought to me,
　　And silken snoods he gae me twa ;
And I will wear them for his sake,
　　The bonnie lad that's far awa.

O, weary winter soon will pass,
　　And spring will cleed the birken-shaw :
And my sweet babie will be born,
　　And he'll come hame that's far awa.

Here's a Health to them that's awa'

Here's a health to them that's awa,
Here's a health to them that's awa ;
And wha winna wish guid luck to our cause,
May never guid luck be their fa' !

4

It's guid to be merry and wise,
It's guid to be honest and true,
It's guid to support Caledonia's cause,
And bide by the buff and the blue.

Here's a health to them that's awa,
Here's a health to them that's awa ;
Here's a health to Charlie, the chief o' the clan,
Altho' that his band be but sma' !
May liberty meet wi' success !
May prudence protect her frae evil !
May tyrants and tyranny tine in the mist,
And wander their way to the devil !

Here's a health to them that's awa,
Here's a health to them that's awa ;
Here's a health to Tammie, the Norland laddie,
That lives at the lug o' the law !
Here's freedom to him that wad read,
Here's freedom to him that wad write !
There's nane ever fear'd that the truth should be heard,
But they wham the truth wad indite.

Here's a health to them that's awa,
An' here's to them that's awa !
Here's to Maitland and Wycombe, let wha does na like 'em
Be built in a hole in the wa' !
Here's timmer that's red at the heart,
Here's fruit that is sound at the core ;
And may he that wad turn the buff and blue coat
Be turn'd to the back o' the door !

Here's a health to them that's awa,
Here's a health to them that's awa ;
Here's to Chieftain M'Leod, a chieftain worth gowd,
Tho' bred amang mountains o' snaw !
Here's friends on baith sides o' the firth,
And friends on baith sides o' the Tweed ;
And wha wad betray old Albion's right,
May they never eat of her bread !

On the Seas and far away

How can my poor heart be glad,
When absent from my sailor lad ?
How can I the thought forego—
He's on the seas to meet the foe ?
Let me wander, let me rove,
Still my heart is with my love ;
Nightly dreams and thoughts by day
Are with him that's far away.

CHORUS

On the seas and far away,
On stormy seas and far away ;
Nightly dreams and thoughts by day
Are aye with him that's far away.

When in summer noon I faint,
As weary flocks around me pant,
Haply in this scorching sun
My sailor's thund'ring at his gun :
Bullets, spare my only joy !
Bullets, spare my darling boy !
Fate, do with me what you may,
Spare but him that's far away !
On the seas, etc.

At the starless midnight hour,
When winter rules with boundless power ;
As the storms the forest tear,
And thunders rend the howling air,
Listening to the doubling roar,
Surging on the rocky shore,
All I can—I weep and pray,
For his weal that's far away.
On the seas, etc.

Peace, thy olive wand extend,
And bid wild War his ravage end,
Man with brother man to meet,
And as a brother kindly greet :

6

Then may Heaven with prosp'rous gales
Fill my sailor's welcome sails,
To my arms their charge convey,
My dear lad that's far away !
    On the seas, etc.

Musing on the Roaring Ocean

MUSING on the roaring ocean
    Which divides my love and me ;
Wearying Heaven in warm devotion,
    For his weal where'er he be.

Hope and fear's alternate billow
    Yielding late to Nature's law ;
Whisp'ring spirits round my pillow
    Talk of him that's far awa.

Ye whom sorrow never wounded,
    Ye who never shed a tear,
Care-untroubled, joy-surrounded,
    Gaudy day to you is dear.

Gentle night, do thou befriend me ;
    Downy sleep, the curtain draw ;
Spirits kind, again attend me,
    Talk of him that's far awa.

The Battle of the Rodney

GIVEN AT A MEETING OF THE DUMFRIESSHIRE VOLUNTEERS, HELD TO COM-
MEMORATE THE ANNIVERSARY OF RODNEY'S VICTORY OVER THE FRENCH,
OFF DOMINICA, APRIL 12, 1782

INSTEAD of a Song, boys, I'll give you a Toast,—
Here's the memory of those on the Twelfth that we lost !
That we *lost*, did I say ? nay, by Heav'n, that we *found*,
For their fame it shall last while the world goes round.
The next in succession, I'll give you the King,
Whoe'er would betray him, on high may he swing !
And here's the grand fabric, our free Constitution,
As built on the base of our great Revolution !
And longer with Politics, not to be cramm'd,
Be Anarchy curs'd, and be Tyranny damn'd ;
And who would to Liberty e'er prove disloyal,
May his son be a hangman, and himself his first trial !

7

The Song of Death

SCENE—*A field of battle.   Time of the day—Evening*
The wounded and dying of the victorious army
are supposed to join in the song

FAREWELL, thou fair day, thou green earth, and ye skies,
  Now gay with the broad setting sun !
Farewell, loves and friendships, ye dear, tender ties,
  Our race of existence is run !

Thou grim King of Terrors, thou life's gloomy foe,
  Go, frighten the coward and slave !
Go, teach them to tremble, fell Tyrant ! but know,
  No terrors hast thou for the brave !

Thou strik'st the dull peasant—he sinks in the dark,
  Nor saves e'en the wreck of a name :
Thou strik'st the young hero—a glorious mark !
  He falls in the blaze of his fame !

In the field of proud honour—our swords in our hands,
  Our King and our Country to save—
While victory shines on life's last ebbing sands,
  O ! who would not die with the brave !

My Heart's in the Highlands

FAREWELL to the Highlands, farewell to the North,
The birthplace of valour, the country of worth ;
Wherever I wander, wherever I rove,
The hills of the Highlands for ever I love.

CHORUS

  My heart's in the Highlands, my heart is not here ;
  My heart's in the Highlands, a-chasing the deer ;
  A-chasing the wild deer, and following the roe,
  My heart's in the Highlands wherever I go.

Farewell to the mountains high cover'd with snow ;
Farewell to the straths and green valleys below ;
Farewell to the forests and wild-hanging woods ;
Farewell to the torrents and loud-pouring floods.
    My heart's in the Highlands, etc.

Ye Jacobites by name

YE Jacobites by name, give an ear, give an ear ;
　　Ye Jacobites by name, give an ear ;
　　　Ye Jacobites by name,
　　　　Your faults I will proclaim,
　　　　　Your doctrines, I maun blame—
　　　　　　You shall hear.

What is right and what is wrang, by the law, by the law ?
　　What is right and what is wrang by the law ?
　　　What is right and what is wrang ?
　　　　A short sword and a lang,
　　　　　A weak arm, and a strang
　　　　　　For to draw.

What makes heroic strife, fam'd afar, fam'd afar ?
　　What makes heroic strife fam'd afar ?
　　　What makes heroic strife ?
　　　　To whet th' assassin's knife,
　　　　　Or hunt a parent's life
　　　　　　Wi' bluidy war.

Then let your schemes alone, in the State, in the State ;
　　Then let your schemes alone in the State ;
　　　Then let your schemes alone,
　　　　Adore the rising sun,
　　　　　And leave a man undone
　　　　　　To his fate.

The Highland Laddie

(Compiled by Burns from a Jacobite Song)

THE boniest lad that e'er I saw,—
　　Bonie laddie, Highland laddie !
Wore a plaid, and was fu' braw,—
　　Bonie Highland laddie !
On his head a bonnet blue,—
　　Bonie laddie, Highland laddie !
His royal heart was firm and true,—
　　Bonie Highland laddie !

9

" Trumpets sound and cannons roar,
   Bonie lassie, Lawland lassie !
And a' the hills wi' echoes roar,
   Bonie Lawland lassie !
Glory, Honour, now invite,
   Bonie lassie, Lawland lassie !
For freedom, and my King to fight,
   Bonie Lawland lassie ! "

" The sun a backward course shall take,
   Bonie laddie, Highland laddie !
Ere aught thy manly courage shake,
   Bonie Highland laddie !
Go ! for yoursel procure renown,
   Bonie laddie, Highland laddie !
And for your lawful King his crown,
   Bonie Highland laddie ! "

The White Cockade

(Adapted from Herd)

MY love was born in Aberdeen,
The bonniest lad that e'er was seen ;
But now he makes our hearts fu' sad—
He takes the field with his White Cockade.

CHORUS

O, he's a ranting, roving lad !
He is a brisk and a bonnie lad !
Betide what may, I will be wed,
And follow the boy wi' the White Cockade.

I'll sell my rock, my reel, my tow,
My guid gray mare and hawkit cow,
To buy mysel a tartan plaid,
To follow the boy wi' the White Cockade.

The young Highland Rover

LOUD blaw the frosty breezes,
    The snaws the mountains cover ;
Like winter on me seizes,
    Since my young Highland Rover
    Far wanders nations over.
Where'er he go, where'er he stray,
    May Heaven be his warden :
Return him safe to fair Strathspey,
    And bonnie Castle Gordon !

The trees now naked groaning,
    Shall soon wi' leaves be hinging,
The birdies dowie moaning,
    Shall a' be blythely singing,
    And every flower be springing.
Sae I'll rejoice the lee-lang day,
    When by his mighty warden
My youth's return'd to fair Strathspey,
    And bonnie Castle Gordon.

Kenmure's on and awa'

O KENMURE'S on and awa, Willie !
    O Kenmure's on and awa !
And Kenmure's lord's the bravest lord
    That ever Galloway saw.

Success to Kenmure's band, Willie !
    Success to Kenmure's band !
There's no a heart that fears a Whig
    That rides by Kenmure's hand.

Here's Kenmure's health in wine, Willie !
    Here's Kenmure's health in wine !
There ne'er was a coward o' Kenmure's bluid,
    Nor yet o' Gordon's line.

O Kenmure's lads are men, Willie !
    O Kenmure's lads are men !
Their hearts and swords are metal true—
    And that their faes shall ken.

They'll live or die wi' fame, Willie !
   They'll live or die wi' fame !
But soon, wi' sounding victorie,
   May Kenmure's lord come hame !

Here's him that's far awa, Willie !
   Here's him that's far awa !
And here's the flower that I love best—
   The rose that's like the snaw !

I am a Son of Mars

I AM a son of Mars, who have been in many wars,
And show my cuts and scars wherever I come ;
This here was for a wench, and that other in a trench,
When welcoming the French at the sound of the drum.
                    Lal de daudle, etc.

My 'prenticeship I pass'd where my leader breath'd his last,
When the bloody die was cast on the heights of Abram ;
I serv'd out my trade when the gallant game was play'd,
And the Morro low was laid at the sound of the drum.
                    Lal de daudle, etc.

I lastly was with Curtis, among the floating batt'ries,
And there I left for witness an arm and a limb :
Yet let my country need me, with Elliot to head me,
I'd clatter on my stumps at the sound of a drum.
                    Lal de daudle, etc.

And now, tho' I must beg, with a wooden arm and leg,
And many a tatter'd rag hanging over my bum,
I'm as happy with my wallet, my bottle, and my callet,
As when I us'd in scarlet to follow a drum.
                    Lal de daudle, etc.

What tho' with hoary locks, I must stand the winter shocks,
Beneath the woods and rocks, oftentimes for a home ;
When the t'other bag I sell, and the t'other bottle tell,
I could meet a troop of hell at the sound of the drum.
                    Lal de daudle, etc.

(*From* "The Jolly Beggars ")

IN PRAISE OF WOMEN

Ae Fond Kiss

AE fond kiss, and then we sever !
Ae fareweel, and then, for ever !
Deep in heart-wrung tears I'll pledge thee,
Warring sighs and groans I'll wage thee.
Who shall say that Fortune grieves him
While the star of hope she leaves him ?
Me, nae cheerfu' twinkle lights me,
Dark despair around benights me.

I'll ne'er blame my partial fancy,
Naething could resist my Nancy ;
But to see her, was to love her ;
Love but her, and love for ever.
Had we never lov'd sae kindly,
Had we never lov'd sae blindly,
Never met—or never parted,
We had ne'er been broken-hearted.

Fare thee weel, thou first and fairest !
Fare thee weel, thou best and dearest !
Thine be ilka joy and treasure,
Peace, enjoyment, love and pleasure !
Ae fond kiss, and then we sever !
Ae fareweel, alas, for ever !
Deep in heart-wrung tears I'll pledge thee,
Warring sighs and groans I'll wage thee !

My Luve is like a Red, Red Rose

O MY luve is like a red, red rose,
  That's newly sprung in June :
O, my luve is like the melodie
  That's sweetly play'd in tune.

As fair art thou, my bonnie lass,
  So deep in luve am I ;
And I will luve thee still, my dear,
  Till a' the seas gang dry.

Till a' the seas gang dry, my dear,
  And the rocks melt wi' the sun :
And I will luve thee still, my dear,
  While the sands o' life shall run.

And fare thee weel, my only luve,
  And fare thee weel awhile !
And I will come again, my luve,
  Tho' it were ten thousand mile.

Flow gently, Sweet Afton

FLOW gently, sweet Afton, among thy green braes,
Flow gently, I'll sing thee a song in thy praise ;
My Mary's asleep by thy murmuring stream,
Flow gently, sweet Afton, disturb not her dream.

Thou stock-dove whose echo resounds thro' the glen,
Ye wild whistling blackbirds in yon thorny den,
Thou green-crested lapwing, thy screaming forbear,
I charge you, disturb not my slumbering fair.

How lofty, sweet Afton, thy neighbouring hills,
Far mark'd with the courses of clear, winding rills ;
There daily I wander as noon rises high,
My flocks and my Mary's sweet cot in my eye.

How pleasant thy banks and green valleys below,
Where wild in the woodlands the primroses blow ;
There oft as mild ev'ning weeps over the lea,
The sweet-scented birk shades my Mary and me.

Ye Banks and Braes o' Bonnie Doon

YE banks and braes o' bonnie Doon,
  How can ye bloom sae fresh and fair !
How can ye chant, ye little birds,
  And I sae weary, fu' o' care !
Thou'lt break my heart, thou warbling bird,
  That wantons thro' the flowering thorn :
Thou minds me o' departed joys,
  Departed—never to return.

Aft hae I rov'd by bonnie Doon,
  To see the rose and woodbine twine ;
And ilka bird sang o' its luve,
  And fondly sae did I o' mine.
Wi' lightsome heart I pu'd a rose,
  Fu' sweet upon its thorny tree ;
And my fause luver stole my rose,
  But ah ! he left the thorn wi' me.

Anna, thy Charms

ANNA, thy charms my bosom fire,
  And waste my soul with care ;
But ah ! how bootless to admire,
  When fated to despair !

Yet in thy presence, lovely fair,
  To hope may be forgiven ;
For sure, 'twere impious to despair
  So much in sight of heaven.

Mary Morison

O MARY, at thy window be,
  It is the wish'd, the trysted hour !
Those smiles and glances let me see,
  That make the miser's treasure poor ;
How blythely wad I bide the stour,
  A weary slave frae sun to sun ;
Could I the rich reward secure,
  The lovely Mary Morison.

Yestreen, when to the trembling string
    The dance gaed thro' the lighted ha',
To thee my fancy took its wing,
    I sat, but neither heard nor saw :
Tho' this was fair, and that was braw,
    And yon the toast of a' the town,
I sigh'd, and said amang them a',
    " Ye are na Mary Morison."

O Mary, canst thou wreck his peace,
    Wha for thy sake wad gladly die ?
Or canst thou break that heart of his,
    Whase only faut is loving thee ?
If love for love thou wilt na gie,
    At least be pity to me shown !
A thought ungentle canna be
    The thought o' Mary Morison.

The Bonnie Lass o' Ballochmyle

'TWAS even, the dewy fields were green,
    On every blade the pearls hang ;
The zephyrs wanton'd round the bean,
    And bore its fragrant sweets alang :
In every glen the mavis sang,
    All Nature listening seem'd the while :
Except where greenwood echoes rang,
    Amang the braes o' Ballochmyle.

With careless step I onward stray'd,
    My heart rejoic'd in Nature's joy,
When musing in a lonely glade,
    A maiden fair I chanc'd to spy ;
Her look was like the morning's eye,
    Her air like Nature's vernal smile,
Perfection whisper'd passing by,
    " Behold the lass o' Ballochmyle ! "

Fair is the morn in flowery May,
    And sweet is night in Autumn mild,
When roving thro' the garden gay,
    Or wandering in the lonely wild :

But Woman, Nature's darling child !
   There all her charms she does compile ;
Ev'n there her other works are foil'd
   By the bonnie lass o' Ballochmyle.

O, had she been a country maid,
   And I the happy country swain,
Tho' shelter'd in the lowest shed
   That ever rose on Scotland's plain,
Thro' weary winter's wind and rain,
   With joy, with rapture, I would toil ;
And nightly to my bosom strain
   The bonnie lass o' Ballochmyle !

Then pride might climb the slipp'ry steep,
   Where fame and honours lofty shine ;
And thirst of gold might tempt the deep,
   Or downward seek the Indian mine ;
Give me the cot below the pine,
   To tend the flocks or till the soil,
And every day have joys divine,
   With the bonnie lass o' Ballochmyle.

Fairest Maid on Devon Banks

FULL well thou know'st I love thee dear,
Couldst thou to malice lend an ear ?
O, did not love exclaim, " Forbear,
   Nor use a faithful lover so " ?

CHORUS

   Fairest maid on Devon banks,
      Crystal Devon, winding Devon,
   Wilt thou lay that frown aside,
      And smile as thou wert wont do to ?

Then come, thou fairest of the fair,
Those wonted smiles, O, let me share ;
And by thy beauteous self I swear,
   No love but thine my heart shall know !
      Fairest maid, etc.

Highland Mary

YE banks and braes and streams around
  The castle o' Montgomery,
Green be your woods, and fair your flowers,
  Your waters never drumlie !
There simmer first unfauld her robes,
  And there the langest tarry ;
For there I took the last fareweel
  O' my sweet Highland Mary.

How sweetly bloom'd the gay green birk,
  How rich the hawthorn's blossom,
As underneath their fragrant shade
  I clasp'd her to my bosom !
The golden hours, on angel wings,
  Flew o'er me and my dearie ;
For dear to me, as light and life,
  Was my sweet Highland Mary.

Wi' monie a vow, and lock'd embrace,
  Our parting was fu' tender ;
And, pledging aft to meet again,
  We tore oursels asunder ;
But oh ! fell Death's untimely frost,
  That nipt my flower sae early !
Now green's the sod, and cauld's the clay,
  That wraps my Highland Mary !

O pale, pale now, those rosy lips,
  I aft hae kiss'd sae fondly !
And closed for aye the sparkling glance,
  That dwelt on me sae kindly !
And mould'ring now in silent dust,
  That heart that lo'ed me dearly !
But still within my bosom's core
  Shall live my Highland Mary.

Anna of the Gowden Locks

YESTREEN I had a pint o' wine,
    A place where body saw na ;
Yestreen lay on this breast o' mine
    The gowden locks of Anna.
The hungry Jew in wilderness,
    Rejoicing o'er his manna,
Was naething to my hinny bliss
    Upon the lips of Anna.

Ye monarchs, tak the east and west,
    Frae Indus to Savannah !
Gie me within my straining grasp
    The melting form of Anna.
There I'll despise imperial charms,
    An Empress or Sultana,
While dying raptures in her arms,
    I give and take with Anna !

Awa, thou flaunting god o' day !
    Awa, thou pale Diana !
Ilk star gae hide thy twinkling ray
    When I'm to meet my Anna.
Come, in thy raven plumage, night,
    Sun, moon, and stars withdrawn a' ;
And bring an angel pen to write
    My transports wi' my Anna !

POSTSCRIPT

The Kirk and State may join, and tell
    To do such things I mauna :
The Kirk and State may gae to Hell,
    And I'll gae to my Anna.
She is the sunshine o' my e'e,
    To live but her I canna ;
Had I on earth but wishes three,
    The first should be my Anna.

Handsome Nell,
or once I lov'd a Bonnie Lass

O ONCE I lov'd a bonnie lass,
  Ay, and I love her still,
And whilst that virtue warms my breast
  I'll love my handsome Nell.

As bonnie lasses I hae seen,
  And monie full as braw,
But for a modest gracefu' mien
  The like I never saw.

A bonnie lass, I will confess,
  Is pleasant to the e'e,
But without some better qualities
  She's no a lass for me.

But Nelly's looks are blithe and sweet,
  And what is best of a',
Her reputation is complete,
  And fair without a flaw.

She dresses aye sae clean and neat,
  Both decent and genteel:
And then there's something in her gait
  Gars onie dress look weel.

A gaudy dress and gentle air
  May slightly touch the heart,
But it's innocence and modesty
  That polishes the dart.

'Tis this in Nelly pleases me,
  'Tis this enchants my soul!
For absolutely in my breast
  She reigns without control.

'Twas na her Bonnie Blue E'e

'Twas na her bonnie blue e'e was my ruin ;
Fair tho' she be, that was ne'er my undoing ;
'Twas the dear smile when naebody did mind us,
'Twas the bewitching, sweet, stown glance o' kindness.

Sair do I fear that to hope is denied me,
Sair do I fear that despair maun abide me ;
But tho' fell Fortune should fate us to sever,
Queen shall she be in my bosom for ever.

Chloris, I'm thine wi' a passion sincerest,
And thou hast plighted me love o' the dearest !
And thou'rt the angel that never can alter,
Sooner the sun in his motion would falter.

Here's to thy Health

Here's to thy health, my bonnie lass,
   Guid night, and joy be wi' thee ;
I'll come nae mair to thy bower door,
   To tell thee that I lo'e thee.
O dinna think, my pretty pink,
   But I can live without thee :
I vow and swear I dinna care
   How lang ye look about ye.

Thou'rt aye sae free informing me
   Thou hast nae mind to marry ;
I'll be as free informing thee
   Nae time hae I to tarry.
I ken thy freens try ilka means
   Frae wedlock to delay thee ;
Depending on some higher chance—
   But fortune may betray thee.

I ken they scorn my low estate,
   But that does never grieve me ;
But I'm as free as any he,
   Sma' siller will relieve me.

I count my health my greatest wealth,
  Sae lang as I'll enjoy it :
I'll fear nae scant, I'll bode nae want,
  As lang's I get employment.

But far aff fowls hae feathers fair,
  And aye until ye try them :
Tho' they seem fair, still have a care,
  They may prove as bad as I am.
But at twal at night, when the moon shines bright,
  My dear, I'll come and see thee ;
For the man that lo'es his mistress weel,
  Nae travel makes him weary.

And I'll awa' to Nannie, O

BEHIND yon hills where Lugar flows,
  'Mang moors an' mosses many, O,
The wintry sun the day has clos'd,
  And I'll awa to Nannie, O.

The westlin' wind blaws loud an' shill ;
  The night's baith mirk and rainy, O :
But I'll get my plaid, an' out I'll steal,
  An' owre the hill to Nannie, O.

My Nannie's charming, sweet, an' young :
  Nae artfu' wiles to win ye, O :
May ill befa' the flattering tongue
  That wad beguile my Nannie, O !

Her face is fair, her heart is true,
  As spotless as she's bonnie, O :
The op'ning gowan, wat wi' dew,
  Nae purer is than Nannie, O.

A country lad is my degree,
  An' few there be that ken me, O ;
But what care I how few they be,
  I'm welcome aye to Nannie, O.

My riches a's my penny-fee,
    An' I maun guide it cannie, O ;
But warl's gear ne'er troubles me,
    My thoughts are a' my Nannie, O.

Our auld guidman delights to view
    His sheep an' kye thrive bonnie, O ;
But I'm as blythe that hauds his pleugh,
    An' has nae care but Nannie, O.

Come weel, come woe, I care na by,
    I'll tak what Heav'n will send me, O ;
Nae ither care in life have I,
    But live, an' love my Nannie, O.

Praise Woman still

"ON MY LORD BUCHAN'S VOCIFERATING IN AN ARGUMENT THAT 'WOMEN MUST ALWAYS BE FLATTERED GROSSLY OR NOT SPOKEN TO AT ALL'"

"PRAISE Woman still," his lordship roars,
    "Deserv'd or not, no matter!"
But thee whom all my soul adores,
    There Flattery cannot flatter!
Maria, all my thought and dream,
    Inspires my vocal shell :
The more I praise my lovely theme,
    The more the truth I tell.

Green grow the Rashes, O

THERE'S nought but care on ev'ry han',
    In ev'ry hour that passes, O ;
What signifies the life o' man,
    An' 'twere na for the lasses, O ?

CHORUS

Green grow the rashes, O ;
    Green grow the rashes, O ;
The sweetest hours that e'er I spend,
    Are spent amang the lasses, O !

23

The warly race may riches chase,
    An' riches still may fly them, O ;
An' tho' at last they catch them fast,
    Their hearts can ne'er enjoy them, O.
        Green grow, etc.

But gie me a cannie hour at e'en,
    My arms about my dearie, O ;
An' warly cares, an' warly men,
    May a' gae tapsalteerie, O !
        Green grow, etc.

For you sae douce, ye sneer at this,
    Ye're nought but senseless asses, O ;
The wisest man the warl' saw,
    He dearly lov'd the lasses, O.
        Green grow, etc.

Auld Nature swears, the lovely dears
    Her noblest work she classes, O ;
Her 'prentice han' she tried on man,
    An' then she made the lasses. O.
        Green grow, etc.

III

SONGS OF WORK

My Father was a Farmer

MY father was a farmer upon the Carrick border, O,
And carefully he bred me, in decency and order O ;
He bade me act a manly part, though I had ne'er a farthing, O,
For without an honest manly heart, no man was worth
    regarding, O.

Then out into the world my course I did determine, O ;
Tho' to be rich was not my wish, yet to be great was charm-
    ing, O :
My talents they were not the worst, nor yet my education, O ;
Resolv'd was I, at least to try, to mend my situation, O.

In many a way, and vain essay, I courted Fortune's favour, O ;
Some cause unseen still stept between, to frustrate each
    endeavour, O :
Sometimes by foes I was o'erpower'd ; sometimes by friends
    forsaken, O ;
And when my hope was at the top, I still was worst mistaken, O.

Then sore harass'd, and tir'd at last, with Fortune's vain
    delusion, O,
I dropt my schemes, like idle dreams, and came to this con-
    clusion, O :
The past was bad, and the future hid ; its good or ill untried, O ;
But the present hour was in my pow'r, and so I would enjoy it, O.

No help, nor hope, nor view had I, nor person to befriend
    me, O ;
So I must toil, and sweat and broil, and labour to sustain
    me, O :
To plough and sow, to reap and mow, my father bred me
    early, O ;
For one, he said, to labour bred, was a match for Fortune
    fairly, O.

Thus all obscure, unknown, and poor, thro' life I'm doom'd
　　to wander, O,
Till down my weary bones I lay in everlasting slumber, O.
No view nor care, but shun whate'er might breed me pain or
　　sorrow, O ;
I live to-day as well's I may, regardless of to-morrow, O.

But cheerful still, I am as well as a monarch in a palace, O,
Tho' Fortune's frown still hunts me down, with all her wonted
　　malice, O :
I make indeed my daily bread, but ne'er can make it farther, O ;
But as daily bread is all I need, I do not much regard her, O.

When sometimes by my labour I earn a little money, O,
Some unforeseen misfortune comes generally upon me, O :
Mischance, mistake, or by neglect, or my good-natur'd
　　folly, O ;
But come what will, I've sworn it still, I'll ne'er be
　　melancholy, O.

All you who follow wealth and power, with unremitting
　　ardour, O,
The more in this you look for bliss, you leave your view the
　　farther, O.
Had you the wealth Potosi boasts, or nations to adore you, O,
A cheerful honest-hearted clown I will prefer before you, O.

My Collier Laddie

(Burns refers to this song as old. No copy, except his MS.,
has been found)

　　" WHARE live ye, my bonnie lass,
　　　And tell me how they ca' ye ? "
　　" My name," she says, " is Mistress Jean,
　　　And I follow the Collier laddie."

　　" See you not yon hills and dales
　　　The sun shines on sae brawlie ?
　　They a' are mine, and they shall be thine,
　　　Gin ye'll leave your Collier laddie !

" An' ye shall gang in gay attire,
Weel buskit up sae gaudy,
And ane to wait on every Hand,
Gin ye'll leave your Collier laddie ! "

" Though ye had a' the sun shines on,
And the earth conceals sae lowly,
I wad turn my back on you and it a',
And embrace my Collier laddie.

" I can win my five pennies in a day,
An' spend it at night fu' brawlie,
And make my bed in the collier's neuk
And lie down wi' my Collier laddie.

" Loove for loove is the bargain for me,
Though the wee cot-house should haud me,
And the warld before me to win my bread—
And fair fa' my Collier laddie ! "

The Ploughman's Life

(Founded on an indelicate old song ; last two stanzas by Burns)

THE ploughman he's a bonnie lad,
His mind is ever true, jo ;
His garters knit below his knee,
His bonnet it is blue, jo.

CHORUS

Then up wi't a', my ploughman lad,
And hey, my merry ploughman ;
Of a' the trades that I do ken,
Commend me to the ploughman.

I hae been east, I hae been west,
I hae been at St. Johnston ;
The bonniest sight that e'er I saw
Was the ploughman laddie dancin'.

Snaw-white stockins on his legs,
And siller buckles glancin' ;
A gude blue bonnet on his head,
And oh, but he was handsome.

Hey, the Dusty Miller

HEY, the dusty miller,
  And his dusty coat ;
He will win a shilling,
  Or he spend a groat.
      Dusty was the coat,
        Dusty was the colour,
        Dusty was the kiss
          That I got frae the miller.

Hey, the dusty miller,
  And his dusty sack ;
Leeze me on the calling
  Fills the dusty peck,
      Fills the dusty peck,
        Brings the dusty siller ;
      I wad gie my coatie
        For the dusty miller.

The Tinker's Song

O MERRY hae I been teethin a heckle,
  An' merry hae I been shapin a spoon !
O, merry hae I been cloutin a kettle,
  An' kissin my Katie when a' was done !
O, a' the lang day I ca' at my hammer,
  An' a' the lang day I whistle an' sing !
O' a' the lang night I cuddle my kimmer,
  An' a' the lang night as happy's a king !

Bitter in dool, I lickit my winnins
  O' marrying Bess, to gie her a slave ;
Blest be the hour she cool'd in her linens,
  And blythe be the bird that sings on her grave !
Come to my arms, my Katie, my Katie,
  An' come to my arms, and kiss me again !
Drucken or sober, here's to thee, Katie,
  And blest be the day I did it again !

The Cooper o' Cuddy

THE Cooper o' Cuddy cam here awa,
He ca'd the girrs out o'er us a',
An' our guidwife has gotten a ca',
   That's angered the silly guidman, O.

CHORUS

  We'll hide the cooper behint the door,
    Behint the door, behint the door,
  We'll hide the cooper behint the door,
    And cover him under a mawn, O.

He sought them out, he sought them in,
Wi' " Deil hae her ! " an' " Deil hae him ! "
But the body he was sae doited and blin',
   He wist na where he was gaun, O.

They cooper'd at e'en, they cooper'd at morn,
Till our guidman has gotten the scorn :
On ilka brow she's planted a horn,
   And swears that there they sall stan', O.

A Ruined Farmer

THE sun he is sunk in the west,
All creatures retirèd to rest,
While here I sit, all sore beset
       With sorrow, grief and woe :
And it's O fickle fortune, O !

The prosperous man is asleep,
Nor hears how the whirlwinds sweep ;
But Misery and I must watch
       The surly tempests blow :
And it's O fickle fortune, O !

There lies the dear partner of my breast,
Her cares for a moment at rest !
Must I see thee, my youthful pride,
       Thus brought so very low ?—
And it's O fickle fortune, O !

There lie my sweet babes in her arms ;
No anxious fear their little hearts alarms ;
But for their sake my heart does ache,
     With many a bitter throe :
And it's O fickle fortune, O !

I once was by Fortune carest,
I once could relieve the distrest ;
Now life's poor support, hardly earn'd,
     My fate will scarce bestow :
And it's O fickle fortune, O !

No comfort, no comfort I have !
How welcome to me were the grave !
But then my wife and children dear—
     O, whither would they go ?
And it's O fickle fortune, O !

O, whither, O, where shall I turn,
All friendless, forsaken, forlorn ?
For, in this world, Rest or Peace
     I never more shall know :
And it's O fickle fortune, O !

My Bonnie Lass, I work in Brass

My bonnie lass, I work in brass,
  A tinkler is my station ;
I've travell'd round all Christian ground
  In this my occupation ;
I've ta'en the gold an' been enroll'd
  In many a noble squadron ;
But vain they search'd, when off I march'd
  To go and clout the cauldron.
       I've ta'en the gold, etc.

Despise that shrimp, that wither'd imp,
  Wi' a' his noise and cap'rin',
And tak a share wi' those that bear
  The budget and the apron ;

And by that stoup, my faith and houp,
   And by that dear Kilbagie,
If e'er ye want, or meet wi' scant,
   May I ne'er weet my craigie.
          And by that stoup, etc.

            (*From* "The Jolly Beggars")

The Gallant Weaver

WHERE Cart rins rowin' to the sea,
By monie a flow'r and spreading tree,
There lives a lad, the lad for me,
   He is a gallant weaver.

Oh I had wooers aught or nine,
   They gied me rings and ribbons fine ;
And I was fear'd my heart would tine,
   And I gied it to the weaver.

My daddie sign'd my tocher-band,
To gie the lad that has the land ;
But to my heart I'll add my hand,
   And gie it to the weaver.

While birds rejoice in leafy bowers ;
While bees delight in opening flowers ;
While corn grows green in simmer showers
   I'll love my gallant weaver.

The Gard'ner wi' his Paidle

(Another version of " Dainty Davie ")

WHEN rosy May comes in wi' flowers,
To deck her gay, green-spreading bowers,
Then busy, busy are the hours—
   The gard'ner wi' his paidle.

The crystal waters gently fa',
The merry birds are lovers a',
The scented breezes round him blaw—
   The gard'ner wi' his paidle.

31

When purple morning starts the hare
To steal upon her early fare ;
Then through the dew he maun repair—
   The gard'ner wi' his paidle.

When day, expiring in the west,
The curtain draws o' Nature's rest,
He flies to her arms he lo'es best—
   The gard'ner wi' his paidle.

Rattlin', Roarin' Willie

O RATTLIN', roarin' Willie,
   O, he held to the fair,
An' for to sell his fiddle,
   An' buy some other ware ;
But parting wi' his fiddle,
   The saut tear blin't his e'e
And rattlin', roarin' Willie,
   Ye're welcome hame to me

O Willie, come sell your fiddle,
   O sell your fiddle sae fine ;
O Willie, come sell your fiddle,
   And buy a pint o' wine !

If I should sell my fiddle,
   The warl' would think I was mad
For monie a rantin' day
   My fiddle and I hae had.

As I cam by Crochallan,
   I cannily keekit ben—
Rattlin', roarin' Willie
   Was sitting at yon board en',
Sitting at yon board en',
   And amang guid companie ;
Rattlin', roarin' Willie,
   Ye're welcome hame to me !

My heart was ance as blythe and free
  As simmer days were lang,
But a bonnie, westlin weaver lad
  Has gart me change my sang.

CHORUS

  To the weaver's gin ye go, fair maids,
    To the weaver's gin ye go ;
  I rede you right gang ne'er at night,
    To the weaver's gin ye go.

My mither sent me to the town,
  To warp a plaiden wab ;
But the weary, weary warpin' o't
  Has gart me sigh and sab.
      To the weaver's, etc.

A bonnie westlin weaver lad
  Sat working at his loom ;
He took my heart as wi' a net,
  In every knot and thrum.
      To the weaver's, etc.

I sat beside my warpin'-wheel,
  And aye I ca'd it roun' ;
But every shot and every knock,
  My heart it gae a stoun.
      To the weaver's, etc.

The moon was sinking in the west
  Wi' visage pale and wan,
As my bonnie westlin weaver lad
  Convoy'd me through the glen.
      To the weaver's, etc.

But what was said, or what was done,
  Shame fa' me gin I tell ;
But oh ! I fear the kintra soon
  Will ken as weel's mysel.
      To the weaver's, etc.

YOUNG Jockey was the blythest lad
  In a' our town or here awa ;
Fu' blythe he whistled at the gaud,
  Fu' lightly danc'd he in the ha' !
He roos'd my een sae bonnie blue,
  He roos'd my waist sae genty sma' ;
An' aye my heart cam to my mou,
  When ne'er a body heard or saw.

My Jockey toils upon the plain,
  Thro' wind and weet, thro' frost and snaw ;
And o'er the lea I leuk fu' fain
  When Jockey's owsen hameward ca .
An' aye the night comes round again,
  When in his arms he taks me a' ;
An' aye he vows he'll be my ain
  As lang's he has a breath to draw.

Bessie and her Spinnin' Wheel

O LEEZE me on my spinnin' wheel,
O leeze me on my rock and reel ;
Frae tap to tae that cleeds me bien,
And haps me fiel and warm at e'en !
I'll set me down and sing and spin,
While laigh descends the simmer sun,
Blest wi' content, and milk and meal—
O leeze me on my spinnin' wheel.

On ilka hand the burnies trot,
And meet below my theekit cot ;
The scented birk and hawthorn white,
Across the pool their arms unite,
Alike to screen the birdie's nest,
And little fishes' caller rest ;
The sun blinks kindly in the biel,
Where blythe I turn my spinnin' wheel.

On lofty aiks the cushats wail,
And echo cons the doolfu' tale ;
The lintwhites in the hazel braes,
Delighted, rival ither's lays :
The craik among the claver hay,
The paitrick whirrin' o'er the ley,
The swallow jinkin' round my shiel,
Amuse me at my spinnin' wheel.

Wi' sma' to sell, and less to buy,
Aboon distress, below envy,
O wha wad leave this humble state,
For a' the pride of a' the great ?
Amid their flarin', idle toys,
Amid their cumbrous, dinsome joys,
Can they the peace and pleasure feel
Of Bessie at her spinnin' wheel ?

Meg o' the Mill

O KEN ye what Meg o' the Mill has gotten,
An' ken ye what Meg o' the Mill has gotten ?
She has gotten a coof wi' a claut o' siller,
And broken the heart o' the barley Miller.

The Miller was strappin', the Miller was ruddy ;
A heart like a lord, and a hue like a lady ;
The Laird was a widdiefu', bleerit knurl ;
She's left the guid fellow and ta'en the churl.

The Miller he hecht her a heart leal and loving ;
The Laird did address her wi' matter mair moving—
A fine pacing horse wi' a clear chainèd bridle,
A whip by her side, and a bonnie side-saddle.

O wae on the siller, it is sae prevailing ;
And wae on the love that is fix'd on a mailen !
A tocher's nae word in a true lover's parle,
But, gie me my love, and a fig for the warl' !

There was a Lass, and she was Fair

THERE was a lass, and she was fair,
  At kirk and market to be seen,
When a' the fairest maids were met,
  The fairest maid was bonnie Jean.

And aye she wrought her mammie's wark,
  And aye she sang sae merrily:
The blythest bird upon the bush
  Had ne'er a lighter heart than she.

But hawks will rob the tender joys
  That bless the little lintwhite's nest;
And frost will blight the fairest flowers,
  And love will break the soundest rest.

Young Robie was the brawest lad,
  The flower and pride of a' the glen;
And he had owsen, sheep, and kye,
  And wanton naigies nine or ten.

He gaed wi' Jeanie to the tryst,
  He danc'd wi' Jeanie on the down;
And lang ere witless Jeanie wist,
  Her heart was tint, her peace was stown.

As in the bosom o' the stream
  The moonbeam dwells at dewy e'en;
So trembling, pure, was tender love,
  Within the breast o' bonnie Jean.

And now she works her mammie's wark,
  And aye she sighs wi' care and pain;
Yet wistna what her ail might be,
  Or what wad mak her weel again.

But didna Jeanie's heart loup light,
  And didna joy blink in her e'e,
As Robie tauld a tale o' love,
  Ae e'enin' on the lily lea?

The sun was sinking in the west,
  The birds sang sweet in ilka grove ;
His cheek to hers he fondly prest,
  And whisper'd thus his tale o' love :—

" O Jeanie fair, I lo'e thee dear ;
  O canst thou think to fancy me ?
Or wilt thou leave thy mammie's cot,
  And learn to tent the farms wi' me ?

" At barn or byre thou shaltna drudge,
  Or naething else to trouble thee ;
But stray amang the heather-bells,
  And tent the waving corn wi' me."

Now what could artless Jeanie do ?
  She had nae will to say him na :
At length she blush'd a sweet consent,
  And love was aye between them twa.

The cardin' o't

I coft a stane o' haslock woo',
  To make a wab to Johnny o't ;
For Johnny is my only jo,
  I lo'e him best of onie yet.
    The cardin' o't, the spinnin' o't ;
      The warpin' o't, the winnin' o't ;
    When ilka ell cost me a groat,
      The tailor staw the lynin' o't.

For though his locks be lyart grey,
  And though his brow be beld aboon ;
Yet I hae seen him on a day,
  The pride of a' the parishen,
    The cardin' o't, the spinnin' o't ;
      The warpin' o't, the winnin' o't ;
    When ilka ell cost me a groat,
      The tailor staw the lynin' o't.

Carron Iron Works

WE cam na here to view your warks
  In hopes to be mair wise,
But only, lest we gang to Hell,
  It may be nae surprise.

But when we tirl'd at your door,
  Your porter dought na hear us ;
Sae may, should we to Hell's yetts come,
  Your billy Satan sair us !

Ye Men of Wit and Wealth

WRITTEN ON A WINDOW IN THE " KING'S ARMS " TAVERN, DUMFRIES

YE men of wit and wealth, why all this sneering
'Gainst poor Excisemen ?   Give the cause a hearing :—
What are your landlords' rent-rolls ?—Taxing ledgers.
What premiers ?   What even monarchs ?—Mighty gaugers !
Nay, what are priests, those seeming godly wise men,
What are they, pray, but spiritual Excisemen ?

Lines at Roslin Inn

MY blessings on ye, honest wife !
  I ne'er was here before :
Ye've wealth o' gear for spoon and knife—
  Heart could not wish for more.

Heaven keep you clear of sturt and strife,
  Till far ayont fourscore,
And by the Lord o' death and life,
  I'll ne'er gae by your door !

Tam the Chapman

As Tam the chapman on a day
Wi' Death forgather'd by the way,
Weel pleas'd, he greets a wight sae famous,
And Death was nae less pleased wi' Thomas,
Wha cheerfully lays down his pack,
And there blaws up a hearty crack ;
His social, friendly, honest heart,
Sae tickled Death they couldna part :
Sae after viewing knives and garters,
Death takes him hame to gie him quarters.

IV

SONGS OF FELLOWSHIP

The Deil's awa' wi' the Exciseman

THE Deil cam fiddlin' thro' the toun,
  And danc'd awa wi' the Exciseman ;
And ilka wife cries, " Auld Mahoun,
  I wish you luck o' the prize, man."

CHORUS

The Deil's awa, the Deil's awa,
  The Deil's awa wi' the Exciseman ;
He's danc'd awa, he's danc'd awa,
  He's danc'd awa wi' the Exciseman.

" We'll mak our maut, we'll brew our drink,
  We'll dance, and sing, and rejoice, man ;
And monie braw thanks to the meikle black Deil
  That danc'd awa wi' the Exciseman."
    The Deil's awa, etc.

" There's threesome reels, and foursome reels,
  There's hornpipes and strathspeys, man ;
But the ae best dance e'er cam to the lan',
  Was—the Deil's awa wi' the Exciseman."
    The Deil's awa, etc.

Address to a Haggis

FAIR fa' your honest, sonsie face,
Great chieftain o' the puddin'-race !
Aboon them a' ye tak your place,
        Painch, tripe, or thairm :
Weel are ye wordy o' a grace
        As lang's my arm.

The groaning trencher there ye fill,
Your hurdies like a distant hill,
Your pin wad help to mend a mill
      In time o' need,
While thro' your pores the dews distil
        Like amber bead.

His knife see rustic Labour dight,
An' cut you up wi' ready slight,
Trenching your gushing entrails bright
        Like onie ditch ;
And then, O what a glorious sight,
         Warm-reekin', rich !

Then, horn for horn, they stretch an' strive,
Deil tak the hindmost ! on they drive,
Till a' their weel-swall'd kytes belyve
        Are bent like drums ;
Then auld guidman, maist like to rive,
        " Be thankit ! " hums.

Is there that o'er his French ragout,
Or olio that wad staw a sow,
Or fricassee wad mak her spew
        Wi' perfect sconner,
Looks down wi' sneering, scornfu' view
        On sic a dinner !

Poor devil ! see him owre his trash,
As feckless as a wither'd rash,
His spindle shank a guid whip-lash,
        His nieve a nit :
Thro' bloody flood or field to dash,
        O how unfit !

But mark the Rustic, haggis-fed,
The trembling earth resounds his tread,
Clap in his walie nieve a blade,
        He'll mak it whissle ;
An' legs, an' arms, an' heads will sned,
        Like taps o' thrissle.

Ye Pow'rs, wha mak mankind your care,
And dish them out their bill o' fare,
Auld Scotland wants nae skinkin' ware
   That jaups in luggies ;
But, if ye wish her gratefu' prayer,
   Gie her a Haggis !

Up in the Morning early

CAULD blaws the wind frae east to west,
 The drift is driving sairly ;
Sae loud and shill's I hear the blast,
 I'm sure it's winter fairly.

CHORUS

Up in the morning's no for me,
 Up in the morning early ;
When a' the hills are cover'd wi' snaw,
 I'm sure it's winter fairly.

The birds sit chittering in the thorn,
 A' day they fare but sparely ;
And lang's the night frae e'en to morn,
 I'm sure, it's winter fairly.
   Up in the morning, etc.

Let half-starved Slaves

LET half-starv'd slaves, in warmer skies,
See future wines, rich-clust'ring, rise ;
Their lot auld Scotland ne'er envies,
   But blythe an' frisky,
She eyes her free-born, martial boys,
   Tak aff their whisky.

What tho' their Phœbus kinder warms,
While fragrance blooms an' beauty charms,
When wretches range, in famish'd swarms,
   The scented groves,
Or hounded forth, dishonour arms
   In hungry droves !

Their gun's a burden on their shouther ;
They downa bide the stink o' powther ;
Their bauldest thought's a hank'ring swither
        To stan' or rin,
Till skelp—a shot—they're aff, a' throw'ther,
        To save their skin.

But bring a Scotsman frae his hill,
Clap in his cheek a Highland gill,
Say, " Such is royal George's will,
        An' *there's* the foe ! "
He has nae thought but how to kill
        Twa at a blow.

Nae cauld, faint-hearted doubtings tease him ;
Death comes, wi' fearless eye he sees him ;
Wi' bluidy han' a welcome gies him ;
        An' when he fa's,
His latest draught o' breathin' lea'es him
        In faint huzzas.

Sages their solemn een may steek,
An' raise a philosophic reek,
An' physically causes seek,
        In clime an' season ;
But tell me Whisky's name in Greek,
        I'll tell the reason.

Scotland, my auld, respected Mither !
Tho' whyles ye moistify your leather,
Till whare ye sit, on craps o' heather,
        Ye tine your dam ;
Freedom and Whisky gang thegither—
        Tak aff your dram ! [1]

      (Postscript to " The Author's Earnest Cry and Prayer ")

[1] An alteration made in the 1794 edition to " Tak aff your whitter " has
been universally neglected.

Address to the Deil

O Prince !   O Chief of many thronèd Pow'rs,
That led th' embattled Seraphim to war.

MILTON

O THOU ! whatever title suit thee,
Auld Hornie, Satan, Nick, or Clootie,
Wha in yon cavern grim an' sootie,
   Clos'd under hatches,
Spairges about the brunstane cootie,
   To scaud poor wretches !

Hear me, auld Hangie, for a wee,
An' let poor damnèd bodies be ;
I'm sure sma' pleasure it can gie,
   Ev'n to a deil,
To skelp an' scaud poor dogs like me,
   An' hear us squeel !

Great is thy pow'r, an' great thy fame ;
Far kend an' noted is thy name ;
An' tho' yon lowin' heugh's thy hame,
   Thou travels far ;
An' faith ! thou's neither lag nor lame,
   Nor blate nor scaur.

Whyles, ranging like a roarin' lion
For prey, a' holes an' corners tryin' ;
Whyles on the strong-wing'd tempest flyin',
   Tirlin' the kirks ;
Whyles, in the human bosom pryin',
   Unseen thou lurks.

I've heard my reverend grannie say,
In lanely glens ye like to stray ;
Or where auld, ruin'd castles, grey,
   Nod to the moon,
Ye fright the nightly wand'rer's way,
   Wi' eldritch croon.

When twilight did my grannie summon,
To say her pray'rs, douce, honest woman !
Aft yont the dyke she's heard you bummin',
                    Wi' eerie drone ;
Or, rustlin', thro' the boortrees comin',
                    Wi' heavy groan.

Ae dreary, windy, winter night,
The stars shot down wi' sklentin' light,
Wi' you, mysel, I gat a fright,
                    Ayont the lough ;
Ye, like a rash-buss, stood in sight,
                    Wi' waving sough.

The cudgel in my nieve did shake,
Each bristl'd hair stood like a stake,
When wi' an eldritch, stoor " Quaick, quaick,"
                    Amang the springs,
Awa ye squatter'd like a drake,
                    On whistling wings.

Let warlocks grim, an' wither'd hags,
Tell how wi' you on ragweed nags,
They skim the muirs, an' dizzy crags,
                    Wi' wicked speed ;
And in kirk-yards renew their leagues,
                    Owre howkit dead.

Thence, countra wives, wi' toil an' pain,
May plunge an' plunge the kirn in vain ;
For, oh ! the yellow treasure's taen
                    By witching skill ;
An' dawtit, twal-pint hawkie's gaen
                    As yell's the bill.

Thence, mystic knots mak great abuse,
On young guidmen, fond, keen, an' crouse ;
When the best wark-lume i' the house,
                    By cantrip wit,
Is instant made no worth a louse,
                    Just at the bit.

45

When thowes dissolve the snawy hoord,
An' float the jinglin' icy-boord,
Then, water-kelpies haunt the foord,
    By your direction,
An' nighted trav'llers are allur'd
    To their destruction.

An' aft your moss-traversing Spunkies
Decoy the wight that late an' drunk is :
The bleezin', curst, mischievous monkies
    Delude his eyes,
Till in some miry slough he sunk is,
    Ne'er mair to rise.

When Masons' mystic word an' grip,
In storms an' tempests raise you up,
Some cock or cat your rage maun stop,
    Or, strange to tell !
The youngest Brother ye wad whip,
    Aff straught to hell.

Lang syne, in Eden's bonnie yard,
When youthfu' lovers first were pair'd
An' all the soul of love they shar'd,
    The raptur'd hour,
Sweet on the fragrant, flow'ry swaird,
    In shady bow'r,—

Then you, ye auld, snick-drawing dog !
Ye came to Paradise incog.
An' play'd on man a cursèd brogue,
    (Black be your fa !)
An' gied the infant warld a shog,
    'Maist ruin'd a'.

D'ye mind that day, when in a bizz,
Wi' reekit duds, an' reestit gizz,
Ye did present your smoutie phiz,
    'Mang better folk,
An' sklented on the man of Uz
    Your spitefu' joke ?

An' how ye gat him i' your thrall,
An' brak him out o' house an' hall,
While scabs an' blotches did him gall,
      Wi' bitter claw,
An' lows'd his ill-tongu'd, wicked scawl,
      Was warst ava ?

But a' your doings to rehearse,
Your wily snares an' fechtin' fierce,
Sin' that day Michael did you pierce,
      Down to this time,
Wad ding a Lallan tongue, or Erse,
      In prose or rhyme.

An' now, auld Cloots, I ken ye're thinkin',
A certain Bardie's rantin', drinkin',
Some luckless hour will send him linkin',
      To your black pit ;
But, faith ! he'll turn a corner jinkin',
      An' cheat you yet.

But, fare you weel, auld Nickie-ben !
O wad ye tak a thought an' men' !
Ye aiblins might—I dinna ken—
      Still hae a stake :
I'm wae to think upo' yon den,
      Ev'n for your sake !

Rantin', Rovin' Robin

THERE was a lad was born in Kyle,
But whatna day o' whatna style,
I doubt it's hardly worth the while
   To be sae nice wi' Robin.

CHORUS

   Robin was a rovin' Boy,
      Rantin' rovin', rantin' rovin' ;
   Robin was a rovin' Boy,
      Rantin', rovin' Robin !

Our monarch's hindmost year but ane
Was five-and-twenty days begun,
'Twas then a blast o' Janwar win'
  Blew hansel in on Robin.

The gossip keekit in his loof,
Quo' scho, " Wha lives will see the proof,
This waly boy will be nae coof,
  I think we'll ca' him Robin."

" He'll hae misfortunes great and sma',
But aye a heart aboon them a' ;
He'll be a credit till us a',
  We'll a' be proud o' Robin."

" But sure as three times three mak nine,
I see by ilka score and line,
This chap will dearly like our kin',
  So leeze me on thee, Robin."

" Guid faith ! " quo' scho, " I doubt you, Sir,
Ye gar the lasses lie aspar,
But twenty fauts ye may hae waur,
  So blessings on thee, Robin ! "

To Mr. John Kennedy

Now Kennedy, if foot or horse
E'er bring you in by Mauchline Corss,
Lord, man ! there's lasses there wad force
    A hermit's fancy,
And down the gate, in faith ! they're worse
    And mair unchancy.

But as I'm sayin' please step to Dow's
And taste sic gear as Johnny brews,
Till some bit callan brings me news
    That you are there,
And if we dinna hae a bouse
    I'se ne'er drink mair.

It's no I like to sit an' swallow,
Then like a swine to puke an' wallow,
But gie me just a true good fallow
                Wi' right ingine,
And spunkie ance to make us mellow,
                And then we'll shine.

Now if ye're ane o' warl's folk,
Wha rate the wearer by the cloak,
An' sklent on poverty their joke,
                Wi' bitter sneer,
Wi' you no friendship I will troke—
                Nor cheap nor dear.

But if, as I'm informèd weel,
Ye hate as ill's the vera Deil,
The flinty heart that canna feel—
                Come, Sir, here's tae you !
Hae, there's my haun', I wiss you weel,
                And guid be wi' you !

The Big-bellied Bottle

No churchman am I for to rail and to write,
No statesman nor soldier to plot or to fight,
No sly man of business contriving a snare,
For a big-bellied bottle's the whole of my care.

The peer I don't envy, I give him his bow ;
I scorn not the peasant, tho' ever so low ;
But a club of good fellows, like those that are there,
And a bottle like this, are my glory and care.

Here passes the squire on his brother—his horse ;
There centum per centum, the cit with his purse ;
But see you the Crown, how it waves in the air,
There a big-bellied bottle still eases my care.

The wife of my bosom, alas ! she did die ;
For sweet consolation to church I did fly ;
I found that old Solomon provèd it fair,
That the big-bellied bottle's a cure for all care.

I once was persuaded a venture to make ;
A letter inform'd me that all was to wreck ;
But the pursy old landlord just waddled up stairs,
With a glorious bottle that ended my cares.

" Life's cares they are comforts," a maxim laid down
By the bard, what d'ye call him, that wore the black
    gown ?
And, faith ! I agree with th' old prig to a hair,
For a big-bellied bottle's a heav'n of a care.

A STANZA ADDED IN A MASON LODGE

Then fill up a bumper, and make it o'erflow,
And honours masonic prepare for to throw ;
May every true Brother of the Compass and Square
Have a big-bellied bottle when harass'd with care !

The Lads o' Thorniebank

A' THE lads o' Thorniebank,
  When they gae to the shore o' Bucky,
They'll step in an' tak a pint
    Wi' Lady Onlie, honest Lucky !
      Lady Onlie, honest Lucky,
        Brews guid ale at shore o' Bucky ;
      I wish her sale for her guid ale,
        The best on a' the shore o' Bucky.

Her house sae bien, her curch sae clean,
  I wat she is a dainty chucky ;
And cheerlie blinks the ingle-gleed
    O' Lady Onlie, honest Lucky !
      Lady Onlie, honest Lucky,
        Brews guid ale at shore o' Bucky ;
      I wish her sale for her guid ale,
        The best on a' the shore o' Bucky.

MacPherson's Farewell

FAREWELL, ye dungeons dark and strong,
    The wretch's destinie :
MacPherson's time will not be long
    On yonder gallows-tree.

CHORUS

    Sae rantingly, sae wantonly,
        Sae dauntingly gaed he ;
    He play'd a spring and danc'd it round,
        Below the gallows-tree.

Oh, what is death but parting breath ?
    On monie a bloody plain
I've dar'd his face, and in this place
    I scorn him yet again !

            Sae rantingly, etc.

Untie these bands from off my hands,
    And bring to me my sword !
And there's no a man in all Scotland,
    But I'll brave him at a word.

            Sae rantingly, etc.

I've liv'd a life of sturt and strife ;
    I die by treacherie :
It burns my heart I must depart
    And not avengèd be.

            Sae rantingly, etc.

Now farewell light, thou sunshine bright,
    And all beneath the sky !
May coward shame distain his name,
    The wretch that dare not die !

            Sae rantingly, etc.

Awa wi' your witchcraft o' beauty's alarms,
The slender bit beauty you grasp in your arms :
O, gie me the lass that has acres o' charms,
O, gie me the lass wi' the weel-stockit farms !

CHORUS

Then hey, for a lass wi' a tocher,
Then hey, for a lass wi' a tocher,
Then hey, for a lass wi' a tocher ;
The nice yellow guineas for me !

Your beauty's a flower in the morning that blows,
And withers the faster, the faster it grows ;
But the rapturous charm o' the bonnie green knowes,
Ilk spring they're new deckit wi' bonnie white yowes.
Then hey, etc.

And e'en when this beauty your bosom has blest,
The brightest o' beauty may cloy, when possest ;
But the sweet yellow darlings wi' Geordie imprest,
The langer ye hae them—the mair they're carest !
Then hey, etc.

Death of Robert Ruisseaux

Now Robin lies in his last lair,
He'll gabble rhyme, nor sing nae mair,
Cauld poverty, wi' hungry stare,
      Nae mair shall fear him :
Nor anxious fear, nor cankert care,
      E'er mair come near him.

To tell the truth, they seldom fash't him,
Except the moment that they crush't him
For sune as chance or fate had husht 'em,
      Tho' e'er sae short,
Then wi' a rhyme or sang he lasht 'em,
      And thought it sport.

Tho' he was bred to kintra wark,
And counted was baith wight and stark,
Yet that was never Robin's mark
      To mak a man ;
But tell him, he was learn'd and clark,
      Ye roos'd him than !

Epitaph on John Dove

INNKEEPER, MAUCHLINE

HERE lies Johnny Pigeon ;
What was his religion
  Wha e'er desires to ken,
To some other warl'
Maun follow the carl,
  For here Johnny Pigeon had nane !

Strong ale was ablution,
Small beer persecution,
  A dram was *memento mori* ;
But a full flowing bowl
Was the saving his soul,
  And port was celestial glory.

Auld Lang Syne

SHOULD auld acquaintance be forgot,
  And never brought to min' ?
Should auld acquaintance be forgot,
  And auld lang syne ?

CHORUS

For auld lang syne, my dear,
  For auld lang syne,
We'll tak a cup o' kindness yet,
  For auld lang syne.

And surely ye'll be your pint-stowp,
　　And surely I'll be mine ;
And we'll tak a cup o' kindness yet
　　For auld lang syne.
　　　　For auld, etc.

We twa hae run about the braes,
　　And pu'd the gowans fine ;
But we've wander'd monie a weary fit
　　Sin' auld lang syne.
　　　　For auld, etc.

We twa hae paidl't i' the burn,
　　From mornin' sun till dine ;
But seas between us braid hae roared
　　Sin' auld lang syne.
　　　　For auld, etc.

And there's a hand, my trusty fiere,
　　And gie's a hand o' thine ;
And we'll tak a right guid-willie waught,
　　For auld lang syne.
　　　　For auld, etc.

O, Willie brew'd a Peck o' Maut

O, WILLIE brew'd a peck o' maut,
　　And Rob and Allan cam to see ;
Three blyther hearts, that lee-lang night,
　　Ye wad na fand in Christendie.

CHORUS

We are na fou, we're nae that fou,
　　But just a drappie in our e'e ;
The cock may craw, the day may daw
　　And aye we'll taste the barley bree.

Here are we met, three merry boys,
　　Three merry boys, I trow, are we ;
And monie a night we've merry been,
　　And monie mae we hope to be !
　　　　We are na fou, etc.

It is the moon, I ken her horn,
   That's blinkin' in the lift sae hie ;
She shines sae bright to wyle us hame,
   But by my sooth she'll wait a wee !
        We are na fou, etc.

What first shall rise to gang awa,
   A cuckold, coward loun is he !
Wha first beside his chair shall fa',
   He is the King amang us three !
        We are na fou, etc.

V

THE FIRESIDE AND NATURE

The Cotter's Saturday Night

INSCRIBED TO ROBERT AIKEN, ESQ., OF AYR

Let not Ambition mock their useful toil,
Their homely joys, and destiny obscure;
Nor Grandeur hear, with a disdainful smile,
The short and simple annals of the Poor.

GRAY

My lov'd, my honour'd, much respected friend !
  No mercenary bard his homage pays ;
With honest pride, I scorn each selfish end,
  My dearest meed, a friend's esteem and praise :
To you I sing, in simple Scottish lays,
  The lowly train in life's sequester'd scene ;
The native feelings strong, the guileless ways ;
  What Aiken in a cottage would have been ;
Ah ! tho' his worth unknown, far happier there, I ween.

November chill blaws loud wi' angry sugh ;
  The short'ning winter-day is near a close ;
The miry beasts retreating frae the pleugh ;
  The black'ning trains o' craws to their repose :
The toil-worn Cotter frae his labour goes,
  This night his weekly moil is at an end,
Collects his spades, his mattocks, and his hoes,
  Hoping the morn in ease and rest to spend,
And weary, o'er the moor, his course does hameward bend.

At length his lonely cot appears in view,
  Beneath the shelter of an agèd tree ;
Th' expectant wee-things, toddlin', stacher through
  To meet their Dad, wi' flickerin' noise an' glee.
His wee bit ingle, blinkin' bonnilie,
  His clean hearth-stane, his thrifty wifie's smile,
The lisping infant prattling on his knee,
  Does a' his weary kiaugh and care beguile,
An' makes him quite forget his labour an' his toil.

Belyve, the elder bairns come drapping in,
    At service out, amang the farmers roun';
Some ca' the pleugh, some herd, some tentie rin
    A cannie errand to a neebor town:
Their eldest hope, their Jenny, woman-grown,
    In youthfu' bloom, love sparkling in her e'e,
Comes hame, perhaps, to show a braw new gown,
    Or deposite her sair-won penny-fee,
To help her parents dear, if they in hardship be.

With joy unfeign'd brothers and sisters meet,
    An' each for other's welfare kindly spiers:
The social hours, swift-wing'd, unnotic'd fleet;
    Each tells the uncos that he sees or hears.
The parents, partial, eye their hopeful years,—
    Anticipation forward points the view:
The mother, wi' her needle an' her sheers,
    Gars auld claes look amaist as weel's the new;
The father mixes a' wi' admonition due.

Their master's an' their mistress's command,
    The younkers a' are warnèd to obey;
An' mind their labours wi' an eydent hand,
    An' ne'er, tho' out o' sight, to jauk or play:—
" An' Oh! be sure to fear the Lord alway,
    An' mind your duty, duly, morn an' night!
Lest in temptation's path ye gang astray,
    Implore His counsel and assisting might:
They never sought in vain that sought the Lord aright!"

But hark! a rap comes gently to the door;
    Jenny, wha kens the meaning o' the same,
Tells how a neebor lad cam o'er the moor,
    To do some errands, and convoy her hame.
The wily mother sees the conscious flame
    Sparkle in Jenny's e'e, and flush her cheek;
Wi' heart-struck, anxious care, inquires his name,
    While Jenny hafflins is afraid to speak;
Weel pleas'd the mother hears, it's nae wild, worthless
    rake.

Wi' kindly welcome, Jenny brings him ben ;
  A strappin' youth, he takes the mother's eye ;
Blythe Jenny sees the visit's no ill ta'en ;
  The father cracks of horses, pleughs, and kye.
The youngster's artless heart o'erflows wi' joy,
  But blate and laithfu', scarce can weel behave ;
The mother, wi' a woman's wiles, can spy
  What makes the youth sae bashfu' an' sae grave ;
Weel pleas'd to think her bairn's respected like the lave.

O happy love ! where love like this is found !
  O heart-felt raptures ! bliss beyond compare !
I've pacèd much this weary, mortal round,
  And sage experience bids me this declare :—
" If Heaven a draught of heavenly pleasure spare,
  One cordial in this melancholy vale,
'Tis when a youthful, loving, modest pair,
  In other's arms breathe out the tender tale,
Beneath the milk-white thorn that scents the ev'ning
    gale."

Is there, in human form, that bears a heart—
  A wretch ! a villain ! lost to love and truth !
That can, with studied, sly, ensnaring art,
  Betray sweet Jenny's unsuspecting youth ?
Curse on his perjur'd arts ! dissembling smooth !
  Are honour, virtue, conscience, all exil'd ?
Is there no pity, no relenting ruth,
  Points to the parents fondling o'er their child ?
Then paints the ruin'd maid, and their distraction wild ?

But now the supper crowns their simple board,
  The halesome parritch, chief o' Scotia's food :
The soupe their only hawkie does afford,
  That 'yont the hallan snugly chows her cood ;
The dame brings forth in complimental mood,
  To grace the lad, her weel-hain'd kebbuck, fell ;
An' aft he's prest, an' aft he ca's it guid ;
  The frugal wifie, garrulous, will tell,
How 'twas a towmond auld, sin' lint was i' the bell.

The cheerfu' supper done, wi' serious face,
   They, round the ingle, form a circle wide ;
The sire turns o'er, wi' patriarchal grace,
   The big ha'-Bible, ance his father's pride :
His bonnet rev'rently is laid aside,
   His lyart haffets wearing thin an bare ;
Those strains that once did sweet in Zion glide,
   He wales a portion with judicious care,
And " Let us worship God ! " he says, with solemn air.

They chant their artless notes in simple guise ;
   They tune their hearts, by far the noblest aim :
Perhaps " Dundee's " wild-warbling measures rise,
   Or plaintive " Martyrs," worthy of the name ;
Or noble " Elgin " beets the heav'nward flame,
   The sweetest far of Scotia's holy lays :
Compar'd with these, Italian trills are tame ;
   The tickl'd ears no heartfelt raptures raise ;
Nae unison hae they with our Creator's praise.

The priest-like father reads the sacred page,
   How Abram was the friend of God on high ;
Or Moses bade eternal warfare wage
   With Amalek's ungracious progeny ;
Or how the royal Bard did groaning lie
   Beneath the stroke of Heaven's avenging ire ;
Or Job's pathetic plaint, and wailing cry ;
   Or rapt Isaiah's wild, seraphic fire ;
Or other holy Seers that tune the sacred lyre.

Perhaps the Christian volume is the theme,
   How guiltless blood for guilty man was shed ;
How He, who bore in Heaven the second name,
   Had not on earth whereon to lay His head ;
How His first followers and servants sped ;
   The precepts sage they wrote to many a land :
How he, who lone in Patmos banishèd,
   Saw in the sun a mighty angel stand ;
And heard great Bab'lon's doom pronounc'd by Heaven's
     command.

Then kneeling down, to Heaven's Eternal King,
   The saint, the father, and the husband prays :
Hope " springs exulting on triumphant wing,"
   That thus they all shall meet in future days :
There ever bask in uncreated rays,
   No more to sigh, or shed the bitter tear,
Together hymning their Creator's praise,
   In such society, yet still more dear ;
While circling Time moves round in an eternal sphere.

Compar'd with this, how poor Religion's pride,
   In all the pomp of method, and of art,
When men display to congregations wide
   Devotion's ev'ry grace, except the heart !
The Power, incens'd, the pageant will desert,
   The pompous strain, the sacerdotal stole ;
But haply, in some cottage far apart,
   May hear, well pleas'd, the language of the soul ;
And in His Book of Life the inmates poor enrol.

Then homeward all take off their sev'ral way ;
   The youngling cottagers retire to rest :
The parent-pair their secret homage pay,
   And proffer up to Heav'n the warm request,
That He who stills the raven's clam'rous nest,
   And decks the lily fair in flow'ry pride,
Would, in the way His wisdom sees the best,
   For them and for their little ones provide ;
But chiefly, in their hearts with grace divine preside.

From scenes like these old Scotia's grandeur springs,
   That makes her lov'd at home, rever'd abroad :
Princes and lords are but the breath of kings,
   " An honest man's the noblest work of God " :
And certès, in fair virtue's heavenly road,
   The cottage leaves the palace far behind ;
What is a lordling's pomp ? A cumbrous load,
   Disguising oft the wretch of human kind,
Studied in arts of hell, in wickedness refin'd !

O Scotia! my dear, my native soil!
 For whom my warmest wish to Heaven is sent!
Long may thy hardy sons of rustic toil
 Be blest with health, and peace, and sweet content!
And, Oh! may Heaven their simple lives prevent
 From luxury's contagion, weak and vile!
Then, howe'er crowns and coronets be rent,
 A virtuous populace may rise the while,
And stand a wall of fire around their much-lov'd Isle.

O Thou! who pour'd the patriotic tide
 That stream'd thro' Wallace's undaunted heart,
Who dar'd to, nobly, stem tyrannic pride,
 Or nobly die, the second glorious part—
(The patriot's God, peculiarly Thou art,
 His friend, inspirer, guardian, and reward!)
O never, never, Scotia's realm desert,
 But still the patriot, and the patriot-bard,
In bright succession raise, her ornament and guard!

Of a' the Airts the Wind can blaw

Of a' the airts the wind can blaw,
 I dearly like the west,
For there the bonnie lassie lives,
 The lassie I lo'e best:
There wild woods grow, and rivers row,
 And monie a hill between;
But day and night my fancy's flight
 Is ever wi' my Jean.

I see her in the dewy flowers,
 I see her sweet and fair:
I hear her in the tunefu' birds,
 I hear her charm the air:
There's not a bonnie flower that springs
 By fountain, shaw, or green;
There's not a bonnie bird that sings,
 But minds me o' my Jean.

To a Mouse

ON TURNING HER UP IN HER NEST WITH THE PLOUGH; NOVEMBER, 1785

WEE, sleekit, cow'rin', tim'rous beastie,
O, what a panic's in thy breastie!
Thou need na start awa sae hasty,
   Wi' bickering brattle!
I wad be laith to rin an' chase thee
   Wi' murd'ring pattle!

I'm truly sorry man's dominion
Has broken Nature's social union,
An' justifies that ill opinion,
   Which makes thee startle,
At me, thy poor, earth-born companion,
   An' fellow-mortal!

I doubt na, whyles, but thou may thieve;
What then? poor beastie, thou maun live!
A daimen icker in a thrave
   'S a sma' request:
I'll get a blessin' wi' the lave,
   And never miss't!

Thy wee bit housie, too, in ruin!
Its silly wa's the win's are strewin'!
An' naething, now, to big a new ane,
   O' foggage green!
An' bleak December's winds ensuin',
   Baith snell an' keen!

Thou saw the fields laid bare and waste,
An' weary winter comin' fast,
An' cozie here, beneath the blast,
   Thou thought to dwell,
Till crash! the cruel coulter past
   Out thro' thy cell.

That wee bit heap o' leaves an' stibble,
Has cost thee mony a weary nibble!
Now thou's turn'd out, for a' thy trouble,
   But house or hald,
To thole the winter's sleety dribble,
   An' cranreuch cauld!

But, Mousie, thou art no thy lane,
In proving foresight may be vain :
The best laid schemes o' mice an' men
        Gang aft a-gley,
An' lea'e us nought but grief an' pain,
        For promis'd joy.

Still thou art blest, compar'd wi' me !
The present only toucheth thee :
But, och ! I backward cast my e'e
        On prospects drear !
An' forward, tho' I canna see,
        I guess an' fear !

To a Mountain Daisy

ON TURNING ONE DOWN WITH THE PLOUGH, IN APRIL, 1786

WEE, modest, crimson-tippèd flow'r,
Thou's met me in an evil hour ;
For I maun crush amang the stoure
        Thy slender stem.
To spare thee now is past my pow'r,
        Thou bonnie gem.

Alas ! it's no thy neebor sweet,
The bonnie lark, companion meet !
Bending thee 'mang the dewy weet,
        Wi' spreckl'd breast,
When upward-springing, blythe, to greet
        The purpling east.

Cauld blew the bitter-biting north
Upon thy early, humble birth ;
Yet cheerfully thou glinted forth
        Amid the storm,
Scarce rear'd above the parent-earth
        Thy tender form.

The flaunting flow'rs our gardens yield,
High shelt'ring woods and wa's maun shield,
But thou, beneath the random bield
        O' clod or stane,
Adorns the histie stibble-field,
        Unseen, alane.

There, in thy scanty mantle clad,
Thy snawie bosom sun-ward spread,
Thou lifts thy unassuming head
                    In humble guise ;
But now the share uptears thy bed,
                    And low thou lies !

Such is the fate of artless maid,
Sweet flow'ret of the rural shade !
By love's simplicity betray'd,
                    And guileless trust,
Till she, like thee, all soil'd, is laid
                    Low i' the dust.

Such is the fate of simple Bard,
On life's rough ocean luckless starr'd !
Unskilful he to note the card
                    Of prudent lore,
Till billows rage, and gales blow hard,
                    And whelm him o'er !

Such fate to suffering worth is giv'n,
Who long with wants and woes has striv'n,
By human pride or cunning driv'n
                    To mis'ry's brink,
Till wrench'd of ev'ry stay but Heaven,
                    He, ruin'd, sink !

Ev'n thou who mourn'st the Daisy's fate,
That fate is thine—no distant date ;
Stern Ruin's ploughshare drives, elate,
                    Full on thy bloom,
Till crush'd beneath the furrow's weight,
                    Shall be thy doom !

On seeing a Wounded Hare

WHICH A FELLOW HAD JUST SHOT AT

INHUMAN man ! curse on thy barb'rous art,
    And blasted be thy murder-aiming eye ;
    May never pity soothe thee with a sigh,
Nor ever pleasure glad thy cruel heart !

Go, live, poor wanderer of the wood and field,
   The bitter little that of life remains ;
   No more the thickening brakes and verdant plains
To thee shall home, or food, or pastime yield.

Seek, mangled wretch, some place of wonted rest,
   No more of rest, but now thy dying bed !
   The sheltering rushes whistling o'er thy head,
The cold earth with thy bloody bosom prest.

Perhaps a mother's anguish adds its woe ;
   The playful pair crowd fondly by thy side ;
   Ah ! helpless nurslings, who will now provide
That life a mother only can bestow ?

Oft as by winding Nith, I, musing, wait
   The sober eve, or hail the cheerful dawn,
   I'll miss thee sporting o'er the dewy lawn,
And curse the ruffian's aim, and mourn thy hapless fate.

Nature's Law

A POEM HUMBLY INSCRIBED TO GAVIN HAMILTON, ESQ.

Great Nature spoke, observant man obeyed.
                        POPE

LET other heroes boast their scars,
   The marks of sturt and strife :
And other Poets sing of wars,
   The plagues of human life ;
Shame fa' the fun ! Wi' sword and gun
   To slap mankind like lumber !
I sing his name and nobler fame,
   Wha multiplies our number.

Great Nature spoke, with air benign,
   " Go on, ye human race !
This lower world I you resign ;
   Be fruitful and increase,

The liquid fire of strong desire
   I've pour'd it in each bosom ;
Here, on this hand, does Mankind stand,
   And there, is Beauty's blossom ! "

The hero of these artless strains,
   A lowly bard was he,
Who sung his rhymes in Coila's plains
   With meikle mirth an' glee ;
Kind Nature's care had given his share,
   Large, of the flaming current ;
And, all devout, he never sought
   To stem the sacred torrent.

He felt the powerful, high behest,
   Thrill, vital, thro' and thro' ;
And sought a correspondent breast,
   To give obedience due ;
Propitious Powers screen'd the young flowr's
   From mildews of abortion ;
And lo ! the bard, a great reward,
   Has got a double portion !

Auld, cantie Coil may count the day,
   As annual it returns,
The third of Libra's equal sway,
   That gave another Burns,
With future rhymes, an' other times,
   To emulate his sire ;
To sing auld Coil in nobler style
   With more poetic fire.

Ye Powers of peace, and peaceful song,
   Look down with gracious eyes ;
And bless auld Coila, large and long,
   With multiplying joys.
Long may she stand to prop the land,
   The flow'r of ancient nations ;
And Burnses spring, her fame to sing,
   To endless generations !

To a Louse

ON SEEING ONE ON A LADY'S BONNET, AT CHURCH

Ha ! whare ye gaun, ye crowlin' ferlie !
Your impudence protects you sairly :
I canna say but ye strunt rarely,
   Owre gauze and lace ;
Tho' faith ! I fear ye dine but sparely
   On sic a place.

Ye ugly, creepin', blastit wonner,
Detested, shunn'd by saunt an' sinner,
How dare ye set your fit upon her,
   Sae fine a lady ?
Gae somewhere else, and seek your dinner
   On some poor body

Swith ! in some beggar's haffet squattle ;
There ye may creep, and sprawl, and sprattle
Wi' ither kindred, jumping cattle,
   In shoals and nations ;
Whare horn nor bane ne'er dare unsettle
   Your thick plantations.

Now haud ye there, ye're out o' sight,
Below the fatt'rels, snug an' tight ;
Na, faith ye yet ! ye'll no be right
   Till ye've got on it,
The vera tapmost, tow'ring height
   O' Miss's bonnet.

My sooth ! right bauld ye set your nose out,
As plump and grey as onie grozet ;
O for some rank, mercurial rozet,
   Or fell, red smeddum,
I'd gie you sic a hearty dose o't,
   Wad dress your droddum !

I wad na been surpris'd to spy
You on an auld wife's flannen toy ;
Or aiblins some bit duddie boy,
   On's wyliecoat ;
But Miss's fine Lunardi ! fie,
   How daur ye do't ?

O, Jenny, dinna toss your head,
An' set your beauties a' abroad !
Ye little ken what cursèd speed
   The blastie's makin' !
Thae winks and finger-ends, I dread,
   Are notice takin' !

O wad some Pow'r the giftie gie us
To see oursels as ithers see us !
It wad frae monie a blunder free us
   And foolish notion :
What airs in dress an' gait wad lea'e us,
   And ev'n devotion !

Address to the Toothache

WRITTEN WHEN THE AUTHOR WAS GRIEVOUSLY TORMENTED
BY THAT DISORDER

MY curse upon your venom'd stang,
That shoots my tortur'd gums alang ;
And thro' my lugs gies monie a twang,
   Wi' gnawing vengeance ;
Tearing my nerves wi' bitter pang,
   Like racking engines !

When fevers burn, or ague freezes,
Rheumatics gnaw, or cholic squeezes ;
Our neighbour's sympathy may ease us,
   Wi' pitying moan ;
But thee—thou hell o' a' diseases,
   Aye mocks our groan !

Adown my beard the slavers trickle !
I throw the wee stools o'er the mickle,
As round the fire the giglets keckle
   To see me loup ;
While, raving mad, I wish a heckle
   Were in their doup.

O a' the numerous human dools,
Ill hairsts, daft bargains, cutty-stools,
Or worthy friends rak'd i' the mools,
          Sad sight to see !
The tricks o' knaves, or fash o' fools,
          Thou bear'st the gree !

Where'er that place be priests ca' hell,
Whence a' the tones o' mis'ry yell,
And rankèd plagues their numbers tell,
          In dreadfu' raw,
Thou, Toothache, surely bear'st the bell
          Amang them a' !

O thou grim mischief-making chiel,
That gars the notes of discord squeel,
Till daft mankind aft dance a reel
          In gore a shoe-thick ;—
Gie a' the faes o' Scotland's weal
          A towmond's toothache.

I Murder hate

FIRST EIGHT LINES WERE INSCRIBED ON A WINDOW-PANE IN
THE GLOBE TAVERN ; THE REMAINING EIGHT WERE ADDED
IN BURNS'S COMMONPLACE BOOK

I MURDER hate by field or flood,
Tho' glory's name may screen us ;
In wars at home I'll spend my blood,
Life-giving wars of Venus :
The deities that I adore
Are social Peace and Plenty ;
I'm better pleased to make one more,
Than be the death of twenty.

I would not die like Socrates,
For all the fuss of Plato ;
Nor would I with Leonidas ;
Nor yet would I with Cato.
The Zealots of the Church and State
Shall ne'er my mortal foes be,
But let me have bold Zimri's fate,
Within the arms of Cozbi.

John Anderson, my Jo

JOHN ANDERSON, my jo, John,
  When we were first acquent,
Your locks were like the raven,
  Your bonnie brow was brent ;
But now your brow is beld, John,
  Your locks are like the snow ;
But blessings on your frosty pow,
  John Anderson, my jo.

John Anderson, my jo, John,
  We clamb the hill thegither ;
And monie a canty day, John,
  We've had wi' ane anither :
Now we maun totter down, John,
  And hand in hand we'll go,
And sleep thegither at the foot,
  John Anderson, my jo.

How Cruel are the Parents

How cruel are the parents
  Who riches only prize,
And to the wealthy booby,
  Poor woman sacrifice !
Meanwhile the hapless daughter
  Has but a choice of strife ;
To shun a tyrant father's hate,
  Become a wretched wife.

The ravening hawk pursuing—
  The trembling dove thus flies ;
To shun impelling ruin
  Awhile her pinions tries ;
Till, of escape despairing—
  No shelter or retreat,
She trusts the ruthless falconer,
  And drops beneath his feet.

A Mother's Lament
for the Death of her Son

FATE gave the word, the arrow sped,
　　And pierc'd my darling's heart;
And with him all the joys are fled
　　Life can to me impart!
By cruel hands the sapling drops,
　　In dust dishonour'd laid:
So fell the pride of all my hopes,
　　My age's future shade.

The mother-linnet in the brake
　　Bewails her ravish'd young;
So I, for my lost darling's sake,
　　Lament the live-day long.
Death, oft I've fear'd thy fatal blow,
　　Now, fond, I bare my breast,
O, do thou kindly lay me low
　　With him I love, at rest!

The Bonnie Wee Thing

BONNIE wee thing, cannie wee thing,
　　Lovely wee thing, wert thou mine,
I wad wear thee in my bosom,
　　Lest my jewel it should tine.

Wishfully I look and languish
　　In that bonnie face o' thine;
And my heart it stounds wi' anguish,
　　Lest my wee thing be na mine.

Wit, and grace, and love, and beauty,
　　In ae constellation shine;
To adore thee is my duty,
　　Goddess o' this soul o' mine!

71

My Wife's a Winsome Wee Thing

SHE is a winsome wee thing,
She is a handsome wee thing,
She is a lo'esome wee thing,
　This sweet wee wife o' mine.

I never saw a fairer,
I never lo'ed a dearer,
And niest my heart I'll wear her,
　For fear my jewel tine.

She is a winsome wee thing,
She is a handsome wee thing,
She is a bonnie wee thing,
　This sweet wee wife o' mine.

The warld's wrack, we share o't,
The warstle and the care o't ;
Wi' her I'll blythely bear it,
　And think my lot divine.

The Auld Man

BUT lately seen in gladsome green
　The woods rejoic'd the day,
Thro' gentle showers the laughing flowers
　In double pride were gay :
But now our joys are fled,
　On winter blasts awa ;
Yet maiden May, in rich array,
　Again shall bring them a' !

But my white pow, nae kindly thowe
　Shall melt the snaws of age ;
My trunk of eild, but buss or bield,
　Sinks in time's wintry rage,
Oh, age has weary days,
　And nights o' sleepless pain !
Thou golden time o' youthfu' prime,
　Why com'st thou not again !

Mark yonder Pomp

MARK yonder pomp of costly fashion,
    Round the wealthy, titled bride :
But when compar'd with real passion,
    Poor is all that princely pride.
    What are their showy treasures ?
    What are their noisy pleasures ?
The gay, gaudy glare of vanity and art :
    The polish'd jewel's blaze
    May draw the wond'ring gaze,
    And courtly grandeur bright
    The fancy may delight,
But never, never can come near the heart.

But did you see my dearest Chloris,
    In simplicity's array ;
Lovely as yonder sweet opening flower is,
    Shrinking from the gaze of day.
    O then, the heart alarming,
    And all resistless charming,
In Love's delightful fetters she chains the willing soul !
    Ambition would disown
    The world's imperial crown ;
    Even Avarice would deny
    His worshipp'd deity,
And feel thro' every vein Love's raptures roll.

O wert thou in the Cauld Blast

O WERT thou in the cauld blast,
    On yonder lea, on yonder lea,
My plaidie to the angry airt,
    I'd shelter thee, I'd shelter thee ;
Or did Misfortune's bitter storms
    Around thee blaw, around thee blaw,
Thy bield should be my bosom,
    To share it a', to share it a'.

Or were I in the wildest waste,
    Sae black an' bare, sae black an' bare,
The desert were a paradise,
    If thou wert there, if thou wert there ;

Or were I monarch o' the globe,
　　Wi' thee to reign, wi' thee to reign,
The only jewel in my crown
　　Wad be my queen, wad be my queen.

The Henpeck'd Husband

Curs'd be the man, the poorest wretch in life,
The crouching vassal to a tyrant wife !
Who has no will but by her high permission ;
Who has not sixpence but in her possession ;
Who must to her his dear friend's secrets tell ;
Who dreads a curtain lecture worse than hell.
Were such the wife had fallen to my part,
I'd break her spirit, or I'd break her heart :
I'd charm her with the magic of a switch,
I'd kiss her maids and kick the perverse bitch.

Epitaph to William Muir

An honest man here lies at rest,
　　As e'er God with His image blest ;
The friend of man, the friend of truth ;
The friend of age and guide of youth :
Few hearts like his with virtue warm'd,
Few heads with knowledge so inform'd :
If there's another world, he lives in bliss ;
If there is none, he made the best of this.

On the Birth of a Posthumous Child

BORN IN PECULIAR CIRCUMSTANCES OF FAMILY DISTRESS

Sweet flow'ret, pledge o' meikle love,
　　And ward o' mony a prayer,
What heart o' stane wad thou na move,
　　Sae helpless, sweet, and fair !

November hirples o'er the lea,
　　Chill, on thy lovely form ;
And gane, alas ! the shelt'ring tree,
　　Should shield thee frae the storm.

May He who gives the rain to pour,
  And wings the blast to blaw,
Protect thee frae the driving show'r
  The bitter frost and snaw !

May He, the friend of woe and want,
  Who heals life's various stounds,
Protect and guard the mother plant,
  And heal her cruel wounds !

But late she flourish'd, rooted fast,
  Fair on the summer morn :
Now, feebly bends she in the blast,
  Unshelter'd and forlorn.

Blest be thy bloom, thou lovely gem,
  Unscath'd by ruffian hand !
And from thee many a parent stem
  Arise to deck our land.

VI

RELIGION AND PHILOSOPHY

Address to the Unco Guid

My son, these maxims make a rule,
  And lump them aye thegither ;
The RIGID RIGHTEOUS *is a fool,*
  The RIGID WISE *anither :*
The cleanest corn that e'er was dight
  May hae some pyles o' caff in ;
So ne'er a fellow-creature slight
  For random fits o' daffin.

  SOLOMON.—Eccles. vii. 16

O YE wha are sae guid yoursel,
  Sae pious and sae holy,
Ye've nought to do but mark and tell
  Your neebours' fauts and folly !
Whase life is like a weel-gaun mill,
  Supply'd wi' store o' water,
The heapit happer's ebbing still,
  And still the clap plays clatter.

Hear me, ye venerable core,
  As counsel for poor mortals,
That frequent pass douce Wisdom's door
  For glaikit Folly's portals ;
I, for their thoughtless, careless sakes,
  Would here propone defences,
Their donsie tricks, their black mistakes,
  Their failings and mischances.

Ye see your state wi' theirs compar'd,
  And shudder at the niffer,
But cast a moment's fair regard,
  What maks the mighty differ ;
Discount what scant occasion gave ;
  That purity ye pride in ;
And (what's aft mair than a' the lave)
  Your better art o' hiding.

Think, when your castigated pulse
    Gies now and then a wallop,
What raging must his veins convulse,
    That still eternal gallop :
Wi' wind and tide fair i' your tail,
    Right on ye scud your sea-way ;
But in the teeth o' baith to sail,
    It maks an unco leeway.

See Social life and Glee sit down,
    All joyous and unthinking,
Till, quite transmugrify'd, they're grown
    Debauchery and Drinking :
O would they stay to calculate
    Th' eternal consequences ;
Or your more dreaded hell to state,
    Damnation of expenses !

Ye high, exalted, virtuous dames,
    Tied up in godly laces,
Before ye gie poor Frailty names,
    Suppose a change o' cases ;
A dear lov'd lad, convenience snug,
    A treacherous inclination—
But, let me whisper i' your lug,
    Ye're aiblins nae temptation.

Then gently scan your brother Man,
    Still gentler sister Woman ;
Tho' they may gang a kennin wrang,
    To step aside is human :
One point must still be greatly dark,
    The moving *Why* they do it ;
And just as lamely can ye mark,
    How far perhaps they rue it.

Who made the heart, 'tis He alone
    Decidedly can try us,
He knows each chord—its various tone,
    Each spring—its various bias :
Then at the balance let's be mute,
    We never can adjust it ;
What's done we partly may compute,
    But know not what's resisted.

O THOU, that in the Heavens dost dwell,
Wha, as it pleases best Thysel',
Sends ane to Heaven and ten to Hell,
   A' for Thy glory,
And no for onie guid or ill
    They've done afore Thee !

I bless and praise Thy matchless might,
Whan thousands Thou hast left in night,
That I am here afore Thy sight,
   For gifts an' grace
A burnin' an' a shinin' light,
    To a' this place.

What was I, or my generation,
That I should get sic exaltation ?
I, wha deserve sic just damnation,
   For broken laws,
Five thousand years 'fore my creation,
    Thro' Adam's cause.

When frae my mither's womb I fell,
Thou might hae plungèd me in Hell,
To gnash my gums, to weep and wail,
   In burnin' lake,
Where damnèd devils roar and yell,
    Chain'd to a stake.

Yet I am here a chosen sample,
To show Thy grace is great and ample ;
I'm here a pillar o' Thy temple,
   Strong as a rock,
A guide, a buckler, and example
    To a' Thy flock.

O Lord, Thou kens what zeal I bear,
When drinkers drink, and swearers swear.
And singin' there and dancin' here,
   Wi' great an' sma' :
For I am keepit by Thy fear,
    Free frae them a'.

But yet, O Lord ! confess I must,
At times I'm fash'd wi' fleshly lust,
An' sometimes too, wi' warldly trust,
      Vile self gets in ;
But Thou remembers we are dust,
        Defil'd in sin.

O Lord ! yestreen, Thou kens, wi' Meg—
Thy pardon I sincerely beg,
O ! may it ne'er be a livin' plague
        To my dishonour,
An' I'll ne'er lift a lawless leg
        Again upon her.

Besides I farther maun allow,
Wi' Lizzie's lass, three times I trow ;
But, Lord, that Friday I was fou,
        When I came near her,
Or else Thou kens Thy servant true
        Wad never steer her.

May be Thou lets this fleshly thorn
Beset Thy servant e'en and morn,
Lest he owre high and proud should turn,
        'Cause he's sae gifted ;
If sae, Thy hand maun e'en be borne,
        Until Thou lift it.

Lord, bless Thy chosen in this place,
For here Thou hast a chosen race ;
But God confound their stubborn face,
        And blast their name,
Wha bring Thy elders to disgrace,
        An' public shame !

Lord, mind Gaw'n Hamilton's deserts,
He drinks, an' swears, an' plays at cartes,
Yet has sae monie takin' arts,
        Wi' great an' sma',
Frae God's ain priest the people's hearts
        He steals awa'.

An' whan we chasten'd him therefore,
Thou kens how he bred sic a splore,

As set the warld in a roar
           O' laughin' at us ;
Curse Thou his basket and his store,
           Kail and potatoes.

Lord, hear my earnest cry an' pray'r,
Against that presbyt'ry o' Ayr ;
Thy strong right hand, Lord, make it bare
           Upo' their heads ;
Lord, visit them, and dinna spare,
           For their misdeeds.

O Lord, my God, that glib-tongu'd Aiken
My very heart and soul are quakin',
To think how we stood sweatin', shakin',
           An' piss'd wi' dread,
While he, wi' hingin' lips an' snakin',
           Held up his head.

Lord, in Thy day of vengeance try him ;
Lord, visit them wha did employ him,
And pass not in Thy mercy by 'em,
           Nor hear their pray'r :
But, for Thy people's sake, destroy 'em,
           And dinna spare.

But, Lord, remember me and mine
Wi' mercies temp'ral and divine,
That I for gear and grace may shine,
           Excell'd by nane,
An' a' the glory shall be Thine,
           Amen, Amen.

Epistle to a Young Friend

MAY, 1786

I LANG hae thought, my youthfu' friend,
    A something to have sent you,
Tho' it should serve nae ither end
    Than just a kind memento ;
But how the subject-theme may gang,
    Let time and chance determine ;
Perhaps, it may turn out a sang,
    Perhaps, turn out a sermon.

Ye'll try the world soon, my lad,
　　And, Andrew dear, believe me,
Ye'll find mankind an unco squad,
　　And muckle they may grieve ye :
For care and trouble set your thought,
　　Ev'n when your end's attained ;
And a' your views may come to nought,
　　Where ev'ry nerve is strained.

I'll no say, men are villains a' ;
　　The real, harden'd wicked,
Wha hae nae check but human law,
　　Are to a few restricked :
But och ! mankind are unco weak,
　　An' little to be trusted ;
If self the wavering balance shake,
　　It's rarely right adjusted !

Yet they wha fa' in fortune's strife,
　　Their fate we should na censure,
For still th' important end of life
　　They equally may answer ;
A man may hae an honest heart,
　　Tho' poortith hourly stare him ;
A man may tak a neebor's part,
　　Yet hae nae cash to spare him.

Aye free, aff han', your story tell,
　　When wi' a bosom crony ;
But still keep something to yoursel
　　Ye scarcely tell to ony.
Conceal yoursel as weel's ye can
　　Frae critical dissection ;
But keek thro' ev'ry other man,
　　Wi' sharpen'd, sly inspection.

The sacred lowe o' weel-plac'd love,
　　Luxuriantly indulge it ;
But never tempt th' illicit rove,
　　Tho' naething should divulge it ;
I wave the quantum o' the sin,
　　The hazard o' concealing ;
But och ! it hardens a' within,
　　And petrifies the feeling !

To catch dame Fortune's golden smile,
    Assiduous wait upon her ;
And gather gear by ev'ry wile
    That's justify'd by honour ;
Not for to hide it in a hedge,
    Nor for a train attendant ;
But for the glorious privilege
    Of being independent.

The fear o' hell's a hangman's whip,
    To haud the wretch in order ;
But where ye feel your honour grip,
    Let that aye be your border :
Its slightest touches, instant pause—
    Debar a' side pretences ;
And resolutely keep its laws,
    Uncaring consequences.

The great Creator to revere,
    Must sure become the creature ;
But still the preaching cant forbear,
    And ev'n the rigid feature :
Yet ne'er with wits profane to range,
    Be complaisance extended ;
An atheist-laugh's a poor exchange
    For Deity offended !

When ranting round in pleasure's ring,
    Religion may be blinded ;
Or if she gie a random sting,
    It may be little minded ;
But when on life we're tempest-driv'n,
    A conscience but a canker—
A correspondence fix'd wi' Heav'n
    Is sure a noble anchor !

Adieu, dear, amiable youth !
    Your heart can ne'er be wanting !
May prudence, fortitude, and truth,
    Erect your brow undaunting !
In ploughman phrase, " God send you speed,"
    Still daily to grow wiser ;
And may ye better reck the rede,
    Than ever did th' adviser !

O thou Dread Pow'r

LYING AT A REVEREND FRIEND'S HOUSE ONE NIGHT, THE AUTHOR LEFT
THE FOLLOWING VERSES IN THE ROOM WHERE HE SLEPT

O THOU dread Pow'r who reign'st above,
 I know Thou wilt me hear;
When for this scene of peace and love,
 I make my pray'r sincere.

The hoary sire—the mortal stroke,
 Long, long, be pleas'd to spare;
To bless his little filial flock,
 And show what good men are.

She, who her lovely offspring eyes
 With tender hopes and fears,
O, bless her with a mother's joys,
 But spare a mother's tears!

Their hope, their stay, their darling youth,
 In manhood's dawning blush;
Bless him, Thou God of love and truth!
 Up to a parent's wish.

The beauteous, seraph sister-band,
 With earnest tears I pray,
Thou know'st the snares on ev'ry hand,
 Guide Thou their steps alway.

When soon or late they reach that coast,
 O'er life's rough ocean driven,
May they rejoice, no wand'rer lost,
 A family in Heaven!

A Prayer, in the Prospect of Death

O THOU unknown, Almighty Cause
 Of all my hope and fear!
In whose dread presence, ere an hour,
 Perhaps I must appear!

83

If I have wander'd in those paths
   Of life I ought to shun ;
As something, loudly in my breast,
   Remonstrates I have done ;

Thou know'st that Thou hast formèd me
   With passions wild and strong ;
And list'ning to their witching voice
   Has often led me wrong.

Where human weakness has come short,
   Or frailty stept aside,
Do Thou, All-Good ! for such Thou art,
   In shades of darkness hide.

Where with intention I have err'd,
   No other plea I have,
But, Thou art good ; and Goodness still
   Delighteth to forgive.

A Bard's Epitaph

Is there a whim-inspirèd fool,
Owre fast for thought, owre hot for rule,
Owre blate to seek, owre proud to snool,
      Let him draw near ;
And owre this grassy heap sing dool,
      And drap a tear.

Is there a Bard of rustic song,
Who, noteless, steals the crowds among,
That weekly this area throng,
      O, pass not by !
But, with a frater-feeling strong,
      Here, heave a sigh.

Is there a man whose judgment clear,
Can others teach the course to steer,
Yet runs, himself, life's mad career,
      Wild as the wave ;
Here pause—and, thro' the starting tear,
      Survey this grave.

The poor Inhabitant below
Was quick to learn and wise to know,
And keenly felt the friendly glow,
        And softer flame ;
But thoughtless follies laid him low,
        And stain'd his name !

Reader, attend ! whether thy soul
Soars Fancy's flights beyond the Pole,
Or darkling grubs this earthly hole
        In low pursuit ;
Know, prudent, cautious self-control
        Is Wisdom's root.

On my Ever-honoured Father

O YE whose cheek the tear of pity stains,
  Draw near with pious rev'rence and attend !
Here lies the loving husband's dear remains,
  The tender father, and the gen'rous friend ;
The pitying heart that felt for human woe ;
  The dauntless heart that fear'd no human pride ;
The friend of man, to vice alone a foe ;
  For " ev'n his failings lean'd to virtue's side."

Remorse

OF all the numerous ills that hurt our peace,
That press the soul, or wring the mind with anguish,
Beyond comparison the worst are those
By our own folly, or our guilt brought on.
In every other circumstance, the mind
Has this to say—" It was no deed of mine " ;
But when to all the evil of misfortune
This sting is added—" Blame thy foolish self ! "
Or worser far, the pangs of keen Remorse ;
The torturing, gnawing consciousness of guilt—
Of guilt, perhaps, where we've involvèd others ;
The young, the innocent, who fondly lov'd us,
Nay, more, that very love their cause of ruin !
O burning hell ! in all thy store of torments,
There's not a keener lash !

G   85

Lives there a man so firm, who, while his heart
Feels all the bitter horrors of his crime,
Can reason down its agonising throbs ;
And, after proper purpose of amendment,
Can firmly force his jarring thoughts to peace ?
O, happy ! happy ! enviable man !
O glorious magnanimity of soul !

Tragic Fragment

ALL devil as I am, a damnèd wretch,
A harden'd, stubborn, unrepenting villain,
Still my heart melts at human wretchedness ;
And with sincere tho' unavailing sighs,
I view the helpless children of distress.
With tears indignant I behold th' oppressor
Rejoicing in the honest man's destruction,
Whose unsubmitting heart was all his crime.
Even you, ye helpless crew, I pity you ;
Ye, whom the seeming good think sin to pity ;
Ye poor, despis'd, abandon'd vagabonds,
Whom Vice, as usual, has turn'd o'er to Ruin,
Oh ! but for kind, tho' ill-requited friends,
I had been driven forth like you forlorn,
The most detested, worthless wretch among you !
O injur'd God ! Thy goodness has endow'd me
With talents passing most of my compeers,
Which I in just proportion have abus'd,
As far surpassing other common villains,
As Thou in natural parts hadst given me more.

To Davie, a Brother Poet

JANUARY—[1785]

IT's hardly in a body's pow'r,
To keep, at times, frae being sour,
    To see how things are shar'd ;
How best o' chiels are whyles in want,
While coofs on countless thousands rant,
    And ken na how to wair't :

But, Davie, lad, ne'er fash your head,
  Tho' we hae little gear,
We're fit to win our daily bread,
  As lang's we're hale and fier :
    " Mair spier na, nor fear na,"
      Auld age ne'er mind a feg ;
    The last o't, the warst o't,
      Is only but to beg.

It's no in titles nor in rank ;
It's no in wealth like Lon'on bank,
  To purchase peace and rest :
It's no in making muckle *mair ;*
It's no in books, it's no in lear,
  To make us truly blest :
If happiness hae not her seat
  And centre in the breast,
We may be wise, or rich, or great,
  But never can be blest :
    Nae treasures, nor pleasures,
      Could make us happy lang;
    The heart aye's the part aye,
      That makes us right or wrang.

Then let us cheerfu', acquiesce ;
Nor make our scanty pleasures less,
  By pining at our state ;
And, even should misfortunes come,
(I, here wha sit, hae met wi' some,
  An's thankfu' for them yet)
They gie the wit of age to youth ;
  They let us ken oursel ;
They mak us see the naked truth,
  The real guid and ill.
    Tho' losses, and crosses,
      Be lessons right severe,
    There's wit there, ye'll get there,
      Ye'll find nae other where.

87

All hail, Religion! Maid divine!

ALL hail, Religion! maid divine!
Pardon a muse sae mean as mine,
Who in her rough imperfect line
        Thus daurs to name thee;
To stigmatise false friends of thine
        Can ne'er defame thee.

Tho' blotch't an' foul wi' monie a stain,
An' far unworthy of thy train,
Wi' trembling voice I tune my strain
        To join wi' those
Who boldly daur thy cause maintain
        In spite o' foes:

In spite o' crowds, in spite o' mobs,
In spite of undermining jobs,
In spite o' dark banditti stabs
        At worth an' merit,
By scoundrels, even wi' holy robes,
        But hellish spirit.

O Ayr! my dear, my native ground!
Within thy presbyterial bound,
A candid lib'ral band is found
        Of public teachers,
As men, as Christians too, renown'd,
        An' manly preachers.

Sir, in that circle you are nam'd;
Sir, in that circle you are fam'd;
An' some, by whom your doctrine's blam'd,
        (Which gies you honour,)
Even, Sir, by them your heart's esteem'd,
        An' winning manner.

Contented wi' Little, and cantie wi' Mair

CONTENTED wi' little, and cantie wi' mair,
Whene'er I forgather wi' Sorrow and Care,
I gie them a skelp as they're creepin' alang,
Wi' a cog o' guid swats, and an auld Scottish sang.

I whiles claw the elbow o' troublesome thought ;
But Man is a sodger, and Life is a faught :
My mirth and guid humour are coin in my pouch,
And my freedom's my lairdship nae monarch dare touch.

A towmond o' trouble, should that be my fa',
A night o' guid fellowship sowthers it a' ;
When at the blythe end of our journey at last,
Wha the deil ever thinks o' the road he has past ?

Blind Chance, let her snapper and stoyte on her way,
Be't to me, be't frae me, e'en let the jade gae :
Come ease, or come travail ; come pleasure or pain,
My warst word is—" Welcome, and welcome again ! "

VII

POLITICS AND SECURITY

Lines to a Gentleman

WHO HAD SENT THE POET A NEWSPAPER AND OFFERED TO
CONTINUE IT FREE OF EXPENSE

KIND Sir, I've read your paper through,
And, faith, to me, 'twas really new !
How guess'd ye, Sir, what maist I wanted ?
This monie a day I've grain'd and gaunted,
To ken what French mischief was brewin' ;
Or what the drumlie Dutch were doin' ;
That vile doup-skelper, Emperor Joseph,
If Venus yet had got his nose off ;
Or how the collieshangie works
Atween the Russians and the Turks ;
Or if the Swede, before he halt,
Would play anither Charles the Twalt :
If Denmark, any body spak o't ;
Or Poland, wha had now the tack o't ;
How cut-throat Prussian blades were hingin' ;
How libbet Italy was singin' ;
If Spaniard, Portuguese, or Swiss,
Were sayin' or takin' aught amiss :
Or how our merry lads at hame,
In Britain's court, kept up the game :
How royal George, the Lord leuk o'er him !
Was managing St. Stephen's quorum ;
If sleekit Chatham Will was livin',
Or glaikit Charlie got his nieve in ;
How Daddie Burke the plea was cookin',
If Warren Hastings' neck was yeukin' ;
How cesses, stents, and fees were rax'd,
Or if bare arses yet were tax'd ;
The news o' princes, dukes, and earls,
Pimps, sharpers, bawds, and opera-girls ;
If that daft buckie, Geordie Wales,
Was threshin' still at hizzies' tails ;

Or if he was grown oughtlins doucer,
And no a perfect kintra cooser.
  A' this and mair I never heard of ;
And, but for you, I might despair'd of.
So gratefu', back your news I send you,
And pray a' guid things may attend you !

Man was made to Mourn

A DIRGE

WHEN chill November's surly blast
  Made fields and forests bare,
One ev'ning as I wander'd forth
  Along the banks of Ayr,
I spy'd a man, whose agèd step
  Seem'd weary, worn with care ;
His face was furrow'd o'er with years,
  And hoary was his hair.

" Young stranger, whither wand'rest thou ? "
  Began the rev'rend Sage ;
" Does thirst of wealth thy step constrain,
  Or youthful pleasure's rage ?
Or, haply, prest with cares and woes,
  Too soon thou hast began
To wander forth, with me, to mourn
  The miseries of Man.

" The sun that overhangs yon moors,
  Out-spreading far and wide,
Where hundreds labour to support
  A haughty lordling's pride ;
I've seen yon weary winter-sun
  Twice forty times return ;
And ev'ry time has added proofs,
  That Man was made to mourn.

" O Man ! while in thy early years,
  How prodigal of time !
Mis-spending all thy precious hours,
  Thy glorious youthful prime !
Alternate follies take the sway ;
  Licentious passions burn ;
Which tenfold force give Nature's law,
  That Man was made to mourn.

91

" Look not alone on youthful prime,
    Or manhood's active might ;
Man then is useful to his kind,
    Supported is his right,
But see him on the edge of life,
    With cares and sorrows worn,
Then Age and Want, oh ! ill-match'd pair !
    Show Man was made to mourn.

" A few seem favourites of fate,
    In pleasure's lap carest ;
Yet, think not all the rich and great
    Are likewise truly blest.
But, oh ! what crowds in ev'ry land
    Are wretched and forlorn ;
Thro' weary life this lesson learn,
    That Man was made to mourn.

" Many and sharp the num'rous ills
    Inwoven with our frame !
More pointed still we make ourselves,
    Regret, remorse, and shame !
And Man, whose heaven-erected face
    The smiles of love adorn,—
Man's inhumanity to man
    Makes countless thousands mourn !

" See yonder poor, o'erlabour'd wight,
    So abject, mean, and vile,
Who begs a brother of the earth
    To give him leave to toil ;
And see his lordly fellow-worm
    The poor petition spurn,
Unmindful, tho' a weeping wife
    And helpless offspring mourn.

" If I'm design'd yon lordling's slave—
    By Nature's law design'd—
Why was an independent wish
    E'er planted in my mind ?
If not, why am I subject to
    His cruelty, or scorn ?
Or why has Man the will and pow'r
    To make his fellow mourn ?

" Yet, let not this too much, my son,
  Disturb thy youthful breast ;
This partial view of human-kind
  Is surely not the last !
The poor, oppressèd, honest man,
  Had never, sure, been born,
Had there not been some recompense
  To comfort those that mourn !

" O Death ! the poor man's dearest friend,
  The kindest and the best !
Welcome the hour my agèd limbs
  Are laid with thee at rest !
The great, the wealthy, fear thy blow,
  From pomp and pleasure torn ;
But, oh ! a blest relief to those
  That weary-laden mourn ! "

The Ode to George Washington
on his first birthday as President

No Spartan tube, no Attic shell,
  No lyre Æolian I awake.
'Tis Liberty's bold note I swell :
  Thy harp, Columbia, let me take !
See gathering thousands, while I sing,
A broken chain, exulting, bring
  And dash it in a tyrant's face,
And dare him to his very beard,
And tell him he no more is fear'd,
  No more the despot of Columbia's race !
A tyrant's proudest insults braved,
They shout a People freed !   They hail an Empire
  sav'd !

Where is man's godlike form ?
  Where is that brow erect and bold,
  That eye that can unmoved behold
The wildest rage, the loudest storm
That e'er created Fury dared to raise ?
Avaunt ! thou caitiff, servile, base,
That tremblest at a Despot's nod,
Yet, crouching under the iron rod,

Canst laud the arm that struck th' insulting blow !
Art thou of man's Imperial line ?
Dost boast that countenance divine ?
   Each skulking feature answers : No !
But come, ye sons of Liberty,
Columbia's offspring, brave as free,
In danger's hour still flaming in the van,
Ye know, and dare maintain, the Royalty of Man !

Alfred, on thy starry throne
   Surrounded by the tuneful choir,
   The Bards that erst have struck the patriot lyre,
   And rous'd the freeborn Briton's soul of fire.
No more thy England own !
Dare injured nations form the great design
   To make detested tyrants bleed ?
   Thy England execrates the glorious deed !
   Beneath her hostile banners waving,
   Every pang of honour braving,
England in thunder calls : " The Tyrant's cause is mine ! "
That hour accurst how did the fiends rejoice,
And Hell thro' all her confines raise th' exulting voice !
That hour which saw the generous English name
Link't with such damned deeds of everlasting shame !

Thee, Caledonia, thy wild heaths among,
Fam'd for the martial deed, the heaven-taught song,
   To thee I turn with swimming eyes !
Where is that soul of Freedom fled ?
Immingled with the mighty dead
   Beneath that hallow'd turf where Wallace lies !
Hear it not, Wallace, in thy bed of death !
   Ye babbling winds, in silence sweep !
   Disturb not ye the hero's sleep,
Nor give the coward secret breath !
Is this the ancient Caledonian form,
Firm as her rock, resistless as her storm ?
Show me that eye which shot immortal hate,
   Blasting the Despot's proudest bearing !
Show me that arm which, nerv'd with thundering fate,
   Braved Usurpation's boldest daring !
Dark-quench'd as yonder sinking star,
No more that glance lightens afar,
That palsied arm no more whirls on the waste of war.

The Slave's Lament

It was in sweet Senegal that my foes did me enthral,
    For the lands of Virginia, O ;
Torn from that lovely shore, and must never see it more,
    And alas I am weary, weary, O !

All on that charming coast is no bitter snow or frost,
    Like the lands of Virginia, O ;
There streams for ever flow, and there flowers for ever blow,
    And alas I am weary, weary, O !

The burden I must bear, while the cruel scourge I fear,
    In the lands of Virginia, O ;
And I think on friends most dear, with the bitter, bitter tear,
    And alas I am weary, weary, O !

Naebody

I hae a wife o' my ain,
    I'll partake wi' naebody ;
I'll tak cuckold frae nane,
    I'll gie cuckold to naebody.

I hae a penny to spend,
    There—thanks to naebody ;
I hae naething to lend,
    I'll borrow frae naebody.

I am naebody's lord,
    I'll be slave to naebody ;
I hae a guid braid sword,
    I'll tak dunts frae naebody.

I'll be merry and free,
    I'll be sad for naebody ;
If naebody care for me,
    I'll care for naebody.

Awa', Whigs, awa'

OUR thrissles flourish'd fresh and fair,
  And bonnie bloom'd our roses ;
But Whigs came like a frost in June,
  And wither'd a' our posies.

CHORUS

Awa, Whigs, awa !
  Awa, Whigs, awa !
Ye're but a pack o' traitor louns,
  Ye'll do nae guid at a'.

Our ancient crown's fa'n in the dust—
  Deil blin' them wi' the stour o't ;
And write their names in his black beuk,
  Wha gae the Whigs the power o't.
    Awa, Whigs, etc.

Our sad decay in Church and State
  Surpasses my descriving ;
The Whigs came o'er us for a curse,
  And we hae done with thriving.
    Awa, Whigs, etc.

Grim vengeance lang has ta'en a nap,
  But we may see him wauken ;
Gude help the day when royal heads
  Are hunted like a maukin !
    Awa, Whigs, etc.

Logan Braes

O LOGAN, sweetly didst thou glide
That day I was my Willie's bride ;
And years sinsyne hae o'er us run,
Like Logan to the simmer sun ;
But now thy flow'ry banks appear
Like drumlie winter, dark and drear,
While my dear lad maun face his faes,
Far, far frae me and Logan Braes.

Again the merry month o' May
Has made our hills and valleys gay ;
The birds rejoice in leafy bowers,
The bees hum round the breathing flowers ;
Blythe morning lifts his rosy eye,
And evening's tears are tears of joy :
My soul, delightless, a' surveys,
While Willie's far frae Logan Braes.

Within yon milk-white hawthorn bush,
Amang her nestlings, sits the thrush ;
Her faithfu' mate will share her toil,
Or wi' his song her cares beguile :
But I wi' my sweet nurslings here,
Nae mate to help, nae mate to cheer,
Pass widow'd nights and joyless days,
While Willie's far frae Logan Braes.

O wae upon you, men o' State,
That brethren rouse to deadly hate !
As ye mak monie a fond heart mourn,
Sae may it on your heads return !
Ye mindna 'mid your cruel joys
The widow's tears, the orphan's cries ;
But soon may Peace bring happy days,
And Willie hame to Logan Braes !

To a Pound Note

WAE worth thy power, thou cursèd leaf !
Fell source o' a' my woe and grief !
For lack o' thee I've lost my lass !
For lack o' thee I scrimp my glass !
I see the children of affliction
Unaided, thro' thy curs'd restriction.
I've seen the oppressor's cruel smile,
Amid his hapless victim's spoil ;
And for thy potence vainly wished,
To crush the villain in the dust.
For lack o' thee I leave this much-lov'd shore,
Never, perhaps, to greet old Scotland more.

97

In Politics if thou wouldst Mix

IN politics if thou wouldst mix,
  And mean thy fortunes be ;
Bear this in mind,—be deaf and blind,
  Let great folk hear and see.

Thanksgiving for Victory

YE hypocrites !   Are these your pranks—
  To murder men and give God thanks ?
Desist for shame ; proceed no further :
  God won't accept your thanks for murther.

A Man's a Man for a' that

Is there, for honest poverty,
  That hangs his head, and a' that ?
The coward slave, we pass him by,
  We dare be poor for a' that !
    For a' that, and a' that,
      Our toils obscure, and a' that ;
    The rank is but the guinea's stamp ;
      The Man's the gowd for a' that !

What tho' on hamely fare we dine,
  Wear hodden grey, and a' that ?
Gie fools their silks, and knaves their wine,
  A man's a Man for a' that !
    For a' that, and a' that,
      Their tinsel show, and a' that ;
    The honest man, tho' e'er sae poor,
      Is King o' men for a' that !

Ye see yon birkie, ca'd a lord,
  Wha struts, and stares, and a' that ?
Tho' hundreds worship at his word,
  He's but a coof for a' that !
    For a' that, and a' that,
      His riband, star, and a' that,
    The man of independent mind,
      He looks and laughs at a' that !

A prince can mak a belted knight,
  A marquis, duke, and a' that ;
But an honest man's aboon his might,
  Guid faith he maunna fa' that !
    For a' that, and a' that,
      Their dignities, and a' that,
    The pith o' sense, and pride o' worth,
      Are higher rank than a' that !

Then let us pray that come it may,
  As come it will for a' that ;
That Sense and Worth, o'er a' the earth,
  May bear the gree, and a' that !
    For a' that, and a' that,
      It's coming yet, for a' that,
    That Man to Man, the warld o'er,
      Shall brothers be for a' that !

GLOSSARY

Aboon, above
Aiblins, perhaps ; possibly
Aik, oak
Ane, one
Aught, eight ; owns
Ayont, beyond

Bane, bone
Beld, bald
Belyve, by and by
Ben, the spence or parlour
Biel, habitation
Bield, shelter
Bill, bull
Billie, good fellow
Birk, birch
Birken shaw, birch wood
Birkie, fellow
Bit, crisis
Bizz, bustle
Blate, shamefaced
Boortree, elder shrub
Braid, broad
Brent, smooth
Brunstane, brimstone
Bumming, buzzing
Buskit, dressed
Buss, bush

Callan, boy
Callet, trull

Cantie, lively, cheerful
Carl, an old man
Cartes, cards
Chiels, young fellows
Clark, clerkly ; learned
Claut, to snatch at
Cleed, to clothe
Coft, bought
Collieshangie, quarrel
Coof, fool ; ninny
Cooser, stallion
Cootie, wooden kitchen dish
Craig, throat
Craigie, dim. of craig
Craik, corncrake
Cranreuch, hoar frost
Crouse, gleefully
Crowlin', crawling
Curch, headdress
Cutty-stool, low stool

Daimen icker, odd ear of corn
Dawtit, petted
Doited, stupefied
Donsie, unlucky ; bothersome
Dool, sorrow
Douce, grave
Dought na, did not
Doup, backside
Dowie, low-spirited

Droddum, breech
Drumly, muddy
Duds, garments
Duddie, ragged
Dunts, blows

Een, eyes
Eild, age
Eldricht, frightful
Eydent, diligent

Fain, fond
Fash, trouble
Fatt'rels, ribbon-ends
Faught, fight
Feg, fig
Fell, the flesh immediately under the skin ; keen ; biting ; nippy ; tasty ; felly, relentless
Ferlie, wonder
Fiel, soft ; smooth
Fier, healthy ; sound ; brother ; friend
Fiere, friend
Fou, tipsy

Gar, to make
Gaunted, yawned
Gear, goods
Giglets, playful children

Gin, if
Girrs, hoops
Gizz, wig
Glaikit, thoughtless
Gowan, daisy
Gowd, gold
Grained, grinned ; groaned
Gree, prize
Grozet, gooseberry

Haffets, temples
Hafflins, partly
Hain'd, spared
Hairst, harvest
Hald, abiding-place
Hale, whole
Hallan, partition
Hammers, fellows
Hansel, gift
Hap, to wrap
Haslock, finest wool
Haud, to hold
Hawkie, white-faced cow
Hecht, foretold
Heckle, rough comb
Heugh, coal pit
Hinny, honey
Hirples, limps
Hizzie, girl
Hoddin grey, homespun
Houp, hope
Howkit, digged

Ilka, every
Ingine, ingenuity
Ingle, fire
Ingle-cheek, fireside
Ingle-gleed, glowing fire

Jauk, to trifle
Jaups, mud splashes
Jinkin', dodging
Jo, sweetheart

Kail, broth ; cabbage
Kebbuck, cheese
Keckle, to cackle
Keek, look ; peep
Kelpie, water-spirit
Kennin, a little
Kimmer, girl
Kintra, country
Kirn, churn
Knowe, hillock
Knurl, dwarf
Kye, cows
Kytes, bellies

Laigh, low
Laithfu', bashful
Lane, alone
Lave, the rest
Lear, lore ; learning
Leeze me, pleased with

Libbet, gelded
Licket, beating
Lint, flax
Lintwhite, linnet
Loof, palm of hand
Lough, lake
Loup, to leap
Lowe, flame
Lug, ear
Luggies, small wooden dishes
  with handles
Lyart, withered

Mailen, farm
Maukin, hare
Maun, must
Maut, malt
Mavis, thrush
Mawn, basket
Meikle, much
Mools, the earth of graves

Naig, nag
Nieves, fists
Niffer, exchange

Ony, any
Oughtlins, anyways
Owre, over ; too
Owsen, oxen

Paidle, hoe
Painch, paunch
Paitrick, partridge
Parle, speech
Pattle, plough-staff
Penny fee, wages
Poortith, poverty
Pow, head

Rash-buss, bush of rushes
Rax'd, stretched out
Rede, warn
Reestit, withered ; singed ;
  stood restive
Rin, run
Rive, to burst
Roos'd, praised
Rozet, ointment

Sab, sob
Sair, sore
Scaur, scare
Scauld, scold
Scawl, shrew
Scho, she
Sconner, to loathe
Shiel, hut
Shill, shrill
Shog, shock
Skelp, slap ; to run
Skinkin', thin
Sklentin', slanting
Smeddum, dust

Snapper, to stumble
Snell, bitter ; biting
Sowther, to solder
Spairges, scatters about
Spier, to ask
Splore, frolic
Sprattle, to struggle
Spunkies, Wills o' the wisp
Stacher'd, staggered
Stark, strong
Staw, to steal
Steek, to close
Stents, dues
Stoor, hoarse
Stour, dust
Stown, stolen
Stoyte, to stagger
Sturt, to molest
Swaird, sward
Swats, ale
Swither, doubt ; fear

Tapsalteerie, topsy-turvy
Tassie, goblet.
Tent, attend to
Tentie, heedful
Thairm, fiddlestrings
Theekit, thatched
Thrave, twenty-four sheaves
Thrissle, thistle
Thrum, birr
Timmer, timber
Tine, to lose
Tint, lost
Tirl'd, knocked
Tirlin', unroofing
Tocher, dowry
Tow, rope
Towmond, twelvemonth
Troke, to exchange
Twal, twelve

Unco, very ; great

Wab, web
Wair't, spend it
Wales, chooses
Walie, waly, ample
Wark-lume, tool
Warlock, wizard
Waught, copious draught
Waur, to fight ; worse
Weel-gaun, well-going
Weet, wet ; dew ; rain
Widdiefu', ill-tempered
Wrack, vex
Wyle, to beguile
Wyliecoat, flannel vest

Yell, barren
Yett, gate
Yeukin, itching
Yont, beyond
Yowe, ewe